Presented to:

From:

Date:

----

100 Devotions
About the Names of God

I AM

DEVOTIONAL

Diane Stortz

Illustrated by Diane Le Feyer

Tommy
NELSON®

A Division of Thomas Nelson Publishers

Published in Nashville, Tennessee, by Tommy Nelson. Tommy Nelson is an imprint of Thomas Nelson. Thomas Nelson is a registered trademark of HarperCollins Christian Publishing, Inc.

Published in association with the Books & Such Literary Management, 52 Mission Circle, Suite 122, PMB 170, Santa Rosa, California 95409, www.booksandsuch.com.

Tommy Nelson titles may be purchased in bulk for educational, business, fund-raising, or sales promotional use. For information, please e-mail SpecialMarkets@ThomasNelson.com.

Unless otherwise noted, Scripture quotations are taken from the ESV® Bible (The Holy Bible, English Standard Version®). Copyright © 2001 by Crossway, a publishing ministry of Good News Publishers. Used by permission. All rights reserved.

Scripture quotations marked AMP or AMPC are from the Amplified® Bible. Copyright © 1954, 1958, 1962, 1964, 1965, 1987 by The Lockman Foundation. Used by permission. (www.Lockman.org)

Scripture quotations marked ICB are from the International Children's Bible®. Copyright © 1986, 1988, 1999, 2015 by Thomas Nelson. Used by permission. All rights reserved.

Scripture quotations marked NKJV are from the New King James Version®. © 1982 by Thomas Nelson. Used by permission. All rights reserved.

Scripture quotations marked NIV are from the Holy Bible, New International Version®, NIV®. Copyright © 1973, 1978, 1984, 2011 by Biblica, Inc.® Used by permission of Zondervan. All rights reserved worldwide. www.zondervan.com. The "NIV" and "New International Version" are trademarks registered in the United States Patent and Trademark Office by Biblica, Inc.®

Scripture quotations marked NLT are from the Holy Bible, New Living Translation. © 1996, 2004, 2007, 2013, 2015 by Tyndale House Foundation. Used by permission of Tyndale House Publishers, Inc., Carol Stream, Illinois 60188. All rights reserved.

Design by Katie Campbell

Any Internet addresses, phone numbers, or company or product information printed in this book are offered as a resource and are not intended in any way to be or to imply an endorsement by Thomas Nelson, nor does Thomas Nelson vouch for the existence, content, or services of these sites, phone numbers, companies, or products beyond the life of this book.

ISBN 978-0-7180-9673-1

Library of Congress Cataloging-in-Publication Data is on file.

Printed in India

23 24 25 REP 10 9 8 7 6 5

For Roman, Bjorn, Reed, Asher, and Solomon.
Trust God always!

—DS

Contents

A Letter to Parents

Welcome to the *I AM Devotional*! As in all my books based on the Bible, my goal for this resource is making God's wonders known to the next generation. Like you, I want my children and grandchildren to know God through His Word. I'm convinced this is a critically important way they will come to love, obey, and trust Him—and He loves them so very much!

The devotions in this book are based on forty of the many names for God, Jesus, and the Holy Spirit found in the Bible. They are written to help children develop understanding of what the names tell us about God, how we should respond, and how we can see those characteristics of God at work in our own lives. (The companion book of Bible stories about these same names of God is called *I AM: 40 Reasons to Trust God*.)

Each devotion includes discussion questions, a prayer, and a Go Deeper Bible verse to explore. Families can work through the book together, and older children can enjoy using the book for grown-up-style devotions on their own.

Either way, my prayer is for Psalm 9:10 be true for you and your children every day: "Those who know your name put their trust in you"!

Diane Stortz
*Making Him known to
the next generation*

Just for Kids

As I was writing this book, I was thinking about you. Yes, you!
I'm so happy *you* can use this book to get to know God better by
learning about His names.

Did you know that God has many different names? He does,
and each one tells us something about Him—what He is like and
what He does. You might even have questions about God, and
His names can help you find the answers you are looking for.

More than anything, learning about God's names leads us to
love and trust Him more and more. And that is always my prayer
for you!

Blessings,

Diane Stortz

Hello, My Name Is _____

God said to Moses, "I AM WHO I AM. When you go to
the people of Israel, tell them, I AM sent me to you."

Exodus 3:14 ICB

At day camp or on a field trip, you have probably worn a name tag. That way teachers can call you by name. They don't have to yell, "Hey, you!"

When God spoke to Moses at the burning bush, He wanted Moses to tell the Israelites that God would save them. "But the people will want to know who sent me," Moses replied. "When they ask, 'What is his name?' what should I say to them?

"I AM WHO I AM," God told Moses. "That is My name forever. Tell the people that I AM sent you to rescue them and bring them out of Egypt."

The burning bush did not burn up—it stayed the same. It didn't change. God doesn't change either. He is always the same. He doesn't need anything. He had no beginning and He has no end. I AM WHO I AM means all those things.

Later on, when the Israelites began to write I AM in their language, they used just four letters—the Hebrew letters for YHWH. We don't really know how this was pronounced. Some people say Yahweh; others say Jehovah. In your Bible you might see LORD instead (with a big capital *L* and smaller capitals for the rest of the word). In this book, we use Jehovah and also LORD.

God doesn't want you to just know *about* Him. He wants you to know Him personally, like you know your friends. Knowing the meaning of all God's names helps us understand who He is. And getting to know God means getting to know the very best friend you will *ever* have!

Thank You, God, that You want us to know You! I want to learn about Your names and get to know You more each day. Amen.

• What's the first thing you usually ask someone new?
• Who is someone you know well? What is that person like?

GO DEEPER

What does Psalm 9:10 say we can do when we know God well—when we know God's name?

What's in a Name?

Those who know your name put their trust in you.

Psalm 9:10

Names can have special meaning. A baby girl born on Christmas might be named Joy or Belle or Starr. A baby boy born during the Super Bowl might be named for the MVP of the game. Nicknames can have meaning too, like Red for someone with auburn hair or Shorty for someone small. Maybe you were named after your great-aunt Gertrude or your great-great-grandfather Percival!

The names of people in the Bible often tell us something about that person. God formed the first man from the dust of the earth, and his name, Adam, is related to a Hebrew word for "dirt" or "land." God allowed Adam to give names to all the animals—that must have been a lot of fun! Adam also gave the first woman her name, Eve, which sounds like the Hebrew word

for "life-giver." Much later, the princess of Egypt found a Hebrew baby floating in a basket in the Nile River. She named him Moses because it sounds like the Hebrew word that means to take something out of the water.

Sometimes people in the Bible got new names. God changed Abram's name to Abraham, which means "father of many." Jesus changed Simon the fisherman's name to Peter, which means "rock," because Peter would be a strong leader in the church.

God's names have meaning too. I AM WHO I AM is the name God told Moses, but the Bible has many other names for God too. As you go through this book and learn more of God's names, you will get to know Him better and trust Him more. And you can start today!

Dear God, thank You that I can get to know You by name! I want to know You better and trust You more. Help me learn about Your names. Amen.

- Have you ever given something or someone a special name? What was it, and why did you choose it?
- Does your name have a meaning? Find out from your parents, or ask them to go online and see.

GO DEEPER

Should we trust God a little or a lot? Read Proverbs 3:5–6.

Getting to Know You

Grow in your knowledge of God.

Ephesians 1:17 NLT

When you meet new friends, you ask their names. Then you want to know more: What activities do they like? What grade are they in school? Where do they live? You want to get to know them better.

Some people have titles or descriptions that go along with their names, like "youth minister" or "Olympic gold medalist." These titles and descriptions tell us more about what these people do and help us get to know them.

It's the same when we are getting to know God.

We might have questions we would like to ask. Is God strong? Is He good? Does He love us all the time, no matter what? Can He tell us how to have a good life? Other people have had these questions too, and in the Bible God answers them. One of the ways He answers them is with His many names and titles. Some of them are:

God All-Powerful
The Lord My Strength
The Good Shepherd
Savior
The Lord My Light

The apostle Paul prayed that Christians would grow to know God more and more. One of the ways we all can do that is to learn about God's names. Then we'll be able to tell people everywhere, "Great is the LORD and greatly to be praised!" (Psalm 48:1). Whom do you know who needs to hear about our wonderful God?

Dear God, You want me to know You and to tell others about You too. Help me do that as I learn more about Your names. Amen.

- If you had a title after your name, what would it be?
- What is one of your questions about God?

GO DEEPER

Where does God want His name to be known? Look in Romans 9:17 to find out.

OMG

You must not use the name of the
Lord your God thoughtlessly.

Exodus 20:7 ICB

After God rescued His people from slavery in Egypt, He promised to always take care of them, and He gave them ten important rules. We call those rules the Ten Commandments. They are all about loving God and loving people.

Rule number four says, "You must not use the name of the Lord your God thoughtlessly" [Exodus 20:7 ICB]. Other translations of that verse tell us not to misuse God's name, or tell us not to take His name in vain. So what exactly does this commandment mean?

Well, first of all, sometimes people say *God* when they are surprised, as if it were an ordinary word. They don't think about God at all when they say it. They could just as easily say *banana* or *cucumber*. That's really using God's name thoughtlessly!

Other times, you might hear people misuse God's name to try to prove that they are telling you the truth about something, even though they're not. But God never lies. In fact, one of His names is God of Truth. He doesn't want His name to be connected with lies!

When you hear God's name used in wrong ways, ask yourself: What does God's name really mean? He is our Father and Creator, and He loves us very much. Thank God for His great name and His goodness, and ask Him to help you always honor His name.

Dear God, thank You for giving us rules that tell us how to love You and love people. Help me to use Your name in right ways. Amen.

- Why do you think someone starts to use God's name thoughtlessly?
- What should you do if you hear someone using God's name in a wrong way?

GO DEEPER

Where should God's name be praised? Psalm 113:3 will tell you.

It Couldn't Just Happen

*In the beginning, God created the
heavens and the earth.*

Genesis 1:1

Did you know that:

- California and Nevada have trees that are nearly five thousand years old?
- An ostrich can run faster than a horse?
- Children have sixty thousand miles of arteries, veins, and capillaries in their bodies?

Our world is amazing! But how did it all get here?

The first chapter of the Bible tells us who created such amazing people, places, and creatures—it was God! (You can read the full story in Genesis 1.) In six days, God made a perfect, beautiful world out of nothing. Each day He added to the world: light, land and sky, plants and trees, the sun, moon, and stars. Then when the world was ready, God added fish and birds, animals, and finally, people: Adam and Eve, the first man and woman!

And on the seventh day, God rested and enjoyed what He had made.

Maybe you have heard someone say that the world and everything in it just happened to form over many, many years by evolution. But that's not what the Bible says.

In Genesis 1:1, the word for God is *Elohim*. That means "the highest, no one better." Our world couldn't just happen! Someone powerful had to think it up and create it. That Someone was God, our Creator.

Do you like to watch the sunset or look up at the moon? Do you like to watch the birds or enjoy the trees or ocean? When you go outside today or look out your window tonight, why not thank God for the world He made? He listens when you talk with Him.

Dear God, You are powerful and wise! You thought up our world, and then You made it happen. Thank You for telling us in the Bible that You created everything. Amen.

- What is one of your favorite things about our world? What do you like about that particular thing?
- God made your body. What's your favorite thing about how God created you?

GO DEEPER

What does our amazing world tell us about God? Find out in Romans 1:20.

You Are Loved

*See how very much our Father loves us, for he
calls us his children, and that is what we are!*

1 John 3:1 NLT

God, your Creator, loves you so much that He never stops thinking about you. In fact, He was thinking about you even before you were born!

King David wrote, "You saw my bones being formed as I took shape in my mother's body. When I was put together there, you saw my body as it was formed. All the days planned for me were written in your book before I was one day old" (Psalm 139:15–16 ICB).

But there's more. God was thinking about you even before He made the world! Even before creation began, God planned to send Jesus to save you! God planned to send Jesus at just the right time to take the punishment for everyone's sin (the ways we disobey God) so we can live with God forever. Everyone who believes Jesus is God's Son becomes part of God's family, one of His forever kids.

Sometimes when things don't go right, you might feel small—like you are just a kid and don't matter. But you *always* matter to God. You always have, and you always will. God is your Creator. He made you, He cares about you, and He sent Jesus to save you. That's how much you matter. That's how much you are loved!

Dear God, I'm so glad to know You love me and I matter to You! Thank You for planning to send Jesus to be my Savior even before the world began! I love You, God. Amen.

- How does it feel to know that God loves you and how much you matter to Him?
- Are there people at school or on your street who need to know they matter to God? How could you tell them about God's love? What would you say?

GO DEEPER

Does God's love ever end? Read 1 Corinthians 13:8.

Every Word

*Whoever asks for a blessing in the land
will be blessed by the God of Truth.*

Isaiah 65:16 GW

How do you feel when someone says mean things and then laughs and says, "Just joking!"?

Someone who does that is not being a good friend. Nobody wants a friend who can't be trusted to tell the truth.

In the garden of Eden, God told Adam and Eve they could eat the fruit of all the trees in the garden except one, the tree of the knowledge of good and evil. Then Satan disguised himself as a snake, and near that special tree, he tempted Eve to believe that God had lied to her. "You won't die if you eat this fruit," Satan said. "Instead, you'll be very wise, like God." (You can read the full story in Genesis 2–3.)

Oh, what a trickster Satan is! God always tells the truth. Satan, the devil, is God's enemy, and he's the one who lies. Adam and Eve learned that lesson the hard way. They both ate the fruit from the tree of the knowledge of good and evil. They knew right away that they had made a terrible mistake. And even though God never stopped loving Adam and Eve, they had to leave the beautiful garden God had made for them, and they would no longer live forever.

God never lies. In fact, He can't! That means we can trust that what God tells us in the Bible is true, because the Bible is His Word. Whenever you read the Bible, God is talking with you, and you can believe what He says.

Believe the Bible is true, and believe that God wants to bless you. He said He will, and He always tells the truth.

Dear God, thank You for Your true words in the Bible. Help me always listen to Your true words and not to Satan's lies. Amen.

- Why would someone tell a lie?
- How can we know what is true?

GO DEEPER

Why does Satan tell us lies? Find the answer in John 8:44.

The Right Tool for the Job

Take up . . . the sword of the Spirit,
which is the word of God.

Ephesians 6:16–17

Could you score a goal at soccer practice without a ball to kick? Could a firefighter put out a fire without a hose and plenty of water? Could a soldier help to win a battle with a feather for a weapon? No way! We all need the right tools for the job.

After Jesus was baptized, He went into the wilderness for forty days. The devil came to tempt Jesus—to try to get Him to do wrong things. But Jesus didn't sin. He won this battle with Satan by using the best tool for the job—the Word of God. He even said God's words out loud to the devil, and the devil left Him alone.

The Word of God, the Bible, is a powerful weapon! That's why the apostle Paul called the Bible the "sword of the Spirit." The Spirit of God helps us use God's Word to fight back when Satan tempts us to do wrong.

If you are about to say something mean, for example, you can remember Psalm 19:14: "May the words of my mouth and the meditation of my heart be pleasing to you, O LORD" (NLT). Or if you want the last chocolate chip cookie for yourself instead of sharing it with your sister, you can remember Philippians 2:3: "When you do things, do not let selfishness or pride be your guide" (ICB).

Satan is God's enemy, and He is our enemy too. But you can use God's true words to help you obey God and not the devil. God's true words are the right tool for the job!

Dear God, thank You for the Bible, Your true words. Help me remember to use Your words when I am tempted to do something wrong. I want to do what pleases You. Amen.

- How do we know what is right and what is wrong? Who gets to decide?
- How can you store up God's words to use as a tool every day?

GO DEEPER

Psalm 119 is all about the Bible, God's Word. Read this famous verse: Psalm 119:11.

Nothing Too Hard

"I am God All-Powerful. Obey me
and do what is right."

Genesis 17:1 ICB

Did you know that:

- If you could drive to the sun at 65 miles per hour, it would take you 163 years to get there?
- Our galaxy, the Milky Way, contains more than 100 billion stars?
- There could be as many galaxies in the universe as there are stars in the Milky Way?

God created the universe, and it is *huge.* God can do anything, even things that seem impossible to us!

God chose Abraham to be the beginning of a family that would become a great nation someday. (This part of Abraham's story is found in Genesis 12–21.) Abraham didn't understand how that could be possible. He didn't have *any* children, and he and his wife were *very* old! But God promised that Abraham and Sarah would have a son and that their family would grow to be as many as the stars in the sky—too many to count! He promised that Abraham's family would be a blessing to the world.

Abraham believed God, even though he had to wait . . . and wait . . . and wait some more . . . before God's promises all came true. Abraham was one hundred years old when his first son, Isaac, was born. Many years later, Abraham's family had grown into an entire nation. And years after that, Jesus was born into Abraham's family to be the Savior of the world.

Because we know God can do anything, we can believe Him as Abraham did. We can trust Him with any problem and wait for His answer, even when waiting is hard. He is God All-Powerful, and He will always do what is best! What do you need to trust Him about today?

Dear God, nothing is too hard for You! Help me trust You to do what is best, and help me wait patiently for Your answers. Amen.

- Why is it hard to wait?
- If you were Abraham waiting for a son, how would you feel while you waited? How would you feel when God's promise came true?

GO DEEPER

Can God turn something bad into something good? Read Romans 8:28 to find out.

Believe It!

*God can do much, much more than
anything we can ask or think of.*

Ephesians 3:20 ICB

Before Jesus came to earth, God spoke to people through messengers called prophets. Moses, Samuel, Isaiah, Jeremiah, Amos, Daniel, and many other prophets told people what God wanted them to know and what He planned to do.

Did those promises come true? Yes, every one!

God gave His prophets lots of promises about Jesus too. Hundreds of years—even thousands of years—before Jesus was born, God promised to send Someone special to make things right again so we could live with God forever. Here are just three of those promises:

- God told Micah this special Person would be born in Bethlehem (Micah 5:2).
- God told Isaiah that He would suffer and die on a cross (Isaiah 53:5).
- God told King David that He would rise again (Psalm 16:10).

Did God's promises about Jesus come true? Yes, every one! Jesus *was* born in Bethlehem, and He gave His life on the cross to pay the penalty for our sin, and then He rose again!

Now Jesus is in heaven, getting a wonderful home ready for us, and God has promised that someday Jesus will come back to reign as King over earth and heaven!

People make promises but can't always keep them. God has the power to keep *all* His promises. He always has, and He always will. So if Jesus is your Savior, believe God's promise that you will live in heaven with Him forever. Jesus is the promised One who came and died and rose again to make that possible. You can believe it!

Dear God, thank You for always keeping Your promises. Thank You for sending Jesus and that someday He will come again! Amen.

- Have you ever made a promise you couldn't keep? What happened?
- What do you think is the best thing about God's promises and power?

GO DEEPER

In Daniel 2:20, read what the prophet Daniel said about God's power.

Sleepless

The one who watches over you . . .
never slumbers or sleeps.

Psalm 121:3–4 NLT

If your dog barks whenever someone's at the door, we say, "That's a good guard dog." The Secret Service guards the president and the White House in Washington, DC, and soldiers keep watch at the Tomb of the Unknown Soldier all day, every day, in any kind of weather. Security guards protect the treasures at museums and the crowds at sporting events and concerts.

What do all these guards have in common? They have to stay awake. No sleeping on the job allowed!

Have you ever been so tired you just . . . couldn't . . . keep . . . your . . . eyes . . . open . . . any . . . longer? Do you have a younger sibling who gets a little cranky if she doesn't get a nap? What about God? Does *He* ever get tired or need to sleep?

No, never. He is God All-Powerful. The Bible says, "The one who watches over you . . . never slumbers or sleeps." He never gets tired. He never needs a nap. He is always "on duty," always seeing, always watching, always caring for you.

And because God never sleeps, you can! King David said, "I go to bed and sleep in peace. Lord, only you keep me safe" [Psalm 4:8 ICB]. Let the twinkling stars at night remind you that God All-Powerful is watching over you.

Dear God, thank You for guarding me with Your great power! You are God All-Powerful, and You keep me safe. Amen.

- Do you think you would make a good guard? Why or why not?
- What could you say about God to help a friend who feels afraid at night?

GO DEEPER

Could anyone else have power like God's power? Find the answer in Jeremiah 10:6.

Everywhere I Go

The name of the city will be "The Lord Is There."

Ezekiel 48:35 NLT

On August 26, 2016, Australian teenager Lachlan Smart became the youngest person ever to fly solo around the world in a single-engine plane. Lachlan began his trip on July 4, 2016. He made twenty-four stops in fifteen countries. As he traveled, he blogged about the people he met and the sights he saw.

In the Bible, a man named Jacob went on a trip by himself far from his home to visit his relatives. (This part of Jacob's story is found in Genesis 28:10–22). He didn't fly an airplane—he walked. He wasn't trying to set a world record. He was actually running away from his extremely angry brother, Esau. But just like Lachlan Smart saw amazing sights on his journey, Jacob did too.

In the wilderness at night, Jacob fell asleep and dreamed. In his dream, he saw a tall ladder, reaching to heaven, with angels going up and down the ladder and God standing at the top. God talked to Jacob in his dream, giving him the same promises He had made to Jacob's grandfather Abraham.

When Jacob woke up, he said, "God is with me in this wilderness! He has been here with me all this time, and I didn't know it!"

There's nowhere you can go that God isn't there. The Bible says, "If I rise with the sun in the east, and settle in the west beyond the sea, even there you would guide me" [Psalm 139:9–10 ICB]. So wherever you are, wherever you go, take a look around for what God might be doing. Remember, He is there!

Dear God, I'm so glad to know You are with me all the time, wherever I go. Thank You that I am always safe with You! Amen.

- What is the longest trip you've ever taken? How far did you travel?
- Why do you think Jacob was surprised that God was with him in the wilderness?

GO DEEPER

Jonah tried to run from God. Where did Jonah end up? Was God there? Read Jonah 1:17 and 2:1, 10.

How Do You Feel?

Give all your worries and cares to
God, for he cares about you.

1 Peter 5:7 NLT

You probably know what emojis are—maybe you have even explained them to your grandparents! Emojis are those little pictures people use in text messages or social media posts—like smiley or frowny faces. Sometimes emojis tell others what we are *doing*, but most of the time they express how we *feel*.

Are you happy? Overjoyed? Disappointed? Lonely? Surprised? Trying to be patient? Nervous? Working? Sleepy? There's an emoji for that!

God understands all our emotions. He made us and our ability to feel. And no matter what we are feeling, God is with us. He doesn't leave us when we are sad or angry or lonely or afraid. One of His names is "The Lord Is There," remember? And Jesus told His followers, "I am with you always" (Matthew 28:20).

Now, sometimes God challenges us to *do something* with our feelings. In the Bible He tells us to be brave when we are afraid, because He is with us. He tells us it is okay to be angry for a little while but not to hurt anyone when we are. If we feel sad, He wants to hear all about it, and when we are anxious, He says, "Give all your worries and cares to God, for he cares about you."

How are you feeling right now? What would your emjoi be? Tell God all about it! He is right there with you.

Dear God, thank You for caring about
all my feelings! Help me tell You about
my feelings every day. Amen.

- What are three emotions you have felt recently? When did
  you feel them?
- What are some things to do when you feel angry, worried,
  or afraid?

GO DEEPER

Can God help us change our feelings? Read Psalm 30:10–12.

What's the Plan?

Lord, my Rock, I call out to you for help.

Psalm 28:1 ICB

Have you ever tasted lemon juice? It makes your mouth pucker! But add some sugar and then some water and ice, and you've got lemonade! Turning something bitter into something good is what we mean when we say, "If life gives you lemons, make lemonade." In the Bible, Joseph is the perfect example. When things went wrong for Joseph, he trusted God, and God turned Joseph's troubles into a sweet surprise ending. (You can find Joseph's story in Genesis 37; 39–47.)

First, Joseph's brothers sold him to traders who took him to Egypt, far from home. The traders sold Joseph as a slave in the house of Potiphar, the king's prison guard. Potiphar's wife got Joseph thrown in prison for something he didn't do. In prison, Joseph explained a mysterious dream to one of the king's servants, but when that servant got out of prison, he forgot all about Joseph for two long years.

Through all this, God was with Joseph. The king's servant finally remembered that Joseph could explain dreams, and the king called Joseph out of prison to explain a dream to him. Then the king made Joseph an important leader over all of Egypt!

When you have troubles and disappointments, you might wonder what's going on. Why did someone steal your bike? Why does your best friend have to move? We don't always get the answers to our questions, but we can be like Joseph, knowing

that God is with us and trusting His plan. Like a strong rock, God keeps us steady when things go wrong.

Is there trouble or disappointment in your life today? Hold on to God, your Rock, and trust Him and His plan.

> Dear God, when problems and disappointments come, You are a steady Rock under my feet, and I will trust Your plan. Amen.

- How does it feel to walk on a rope bridge or a trampoline? On a concrete or stone path? Which is steadier?
- What problem or disappointment have you had recently? Has anything good come from it yet?

GO DEEPER

What sure-footed animal did David compare himself to after God rescued him from trouble? Read 2 Samuel 22:34.

Let It Go

*May the words from my mouth and the
thoughts from my heart be acceptable to
you, O LORD, my rock and my defender.*

Psalm 19:14 GW

When Frederick Ndabaramiye was a boy in the African country of Rwanda, a terrible war began in his country. Frederick lost his hands and nearly died. But God took care of Frederick, and eventually he began working to help other people with disabilities. In the United States, he received artificial hands. Then, back in Rwanda, Frederick came face-to-face with one of the men who had hurt him. Frederick panicked. All the bad memories came back. He wondered what to do.

Frederick *forgave* the man. And when he did, Frederick felt free. He let go of the heavy grudge in his heart. Joseph would have understood. Remember Joseph's story? His brothers sold him to traders who took him far from home. Joseph had a hard life for many years after that, but God was his strong Rock through all his troubles.

After Joseph became a ruler in Egypt, his brothers came to Egypt to buy grain. They didn't recognize him.

But when they found out he was their brother, they were afraid. What would he do to them?

Joseph forgave them! "You meant to hurt me," he said, "but God meant it for good." God used Joseph in Egypt to save many lives from famine.

Forgiving doesn't mean that what someone did was okay. It means that instead of holding a grudge, we depend on God as our strong Rock to take care of us.

Is there someone you need to forgive? Maybe a bully at school or a friend who hurt your feelings? Decide today not to hold a grudge. Instead, be like Joseph and depend on God, your steady Rock, to take care of you and help you forgive.

Dear God, thank You for showing me how to forgive. Help me not to hold grudges but to always depend on You, my Rock. Amen.

- How does it feel to forgive someone?
- How does it feel when someone forgives you?

GO DEEPER

What did Jesus say on the cross about forgiveness? Look in Luke 23:34.

Holy Ground

God said to Moses, "I AM WHO I AM. When you go to the people of Israel, tell them, "I AM sent me to you.""

Exodus 3:14 ICB

Are there places you go that are special to you? Maybe a lake where you water ski every summer, or your grandfather's beautiful garden, or your neighborhood's soccer field? Places become special to us because of what happens there.

Something special happened in the wilderness where Moses cared for his family's sheep. Moses saw a bush on fire but not burning up—and God talked to Moses there. He had a big, important job for Moses. (You can read all about this in Exodus 3–4.)

"Take off your sandals," God told Moses, "because you are standing on holy ground."

Holy means "set apart." This place was holy because God was there to talk with Moses and because God Himself is holy— He is different from us. He is the Creator. He is always good. He never changes. He is the great I Am.

Because God is holy, He deserves our worship—our praise and our obedience—wherever we are. We can worship by the way we live every day. Have you ever felt like yelling mean, angry words at a younger child who tears apart your best Lego creation? If you remember what God wants and choose to be kind even though you are upset, you are worshiping. You are standing on holy ground!

The Bible says, "Offer your lives as a living sacrifice to him. . . . This is the spiritual way for you to worship" [Romans 12:1 ICB]. How will you worship God today?

Dear God, thank You that I can worship
You every day. Help me to worship
by choosing to do what pleases You.
You are holy and good. Amen.

- How do you think Moses felt when he realized God was talking with him at the burning bush?
- Is it easy or hard to choose to do the things that please God? Why?

GO DEEPER

What does Hebrews 12:28 tell us about how to worship God?

Who, Me?

"Don't worry, because I am with you. Don't
be afraid, because I am your God."

Isaiah 41:10 ICB

Nick Vujicic (pronounced VOO-yee-cheech) once thought his life was just too hard. Nick was born in 1982 without arms or legs. Think about the things you do every day and how difficult it would be to do them if you had no arms or legs! But Nick learned to depend on God to help him live every day, and he even learned to paint, fish, and play golf. Today he speaks around the world, bringing hope to people who feel hopeless.

At the burning bush, Moses got an assignment from God that he thought was just too hard to obey. God had chosen him to lead the His people, the Hebrews, out of Egypt. "I'm not a good speaker," Moses said. "Please send someone else."

"I will be with you," God told Moses. "I will help you. I made your mouth, and I will teach you what to say. And I will send your brother Aaron to help you too."

Did Moses obey? Did he do the hard job from God? Yes! With God's help and strength, and some help from his brother, Moses led the people out of Egypt, through the Red Sea, and toward the Promised Land.

Can you do a hard job with God to help you? Yes, you can. Are you facing a big test at school? Are you trying to make the gymnastics team? Do you have to move because a parent got a new job in a different state? Do you want to tell a new friend about Jesus? God, I AM WHO I AM, can do anything, and He will help you obey Him and do hard things. Why not ask Him for His help right now?

Dear God, when I need to obey or do something hard, help me remember that You are with me and will help me. Thank You, God! Amen.

- What are some hard things you have had to do? How did you do them?
- Why is it sometimes hard to obey God? How can God help us with hard things?

GO DEEPER

Is there anything too hard for God? Read Luke 1:37.

Special Delivery

Our God is a God who saves us.

Psalm 68:20 ICB

How many push-ups can you do? How many sit-ups? Physical fitness is one type of strength, but there are other ways to be strong too. If you're good at arithmetic and solving word problems, you're strong in math. If you are great at catching fly balls, you're strong on the baseball field.

Remember Joseph and his father, Jacob? When Jacob and his sons and their families came to live in in Egypt, the king was kind to them. But Jacob's family grew and grew. They were called the Hebrews. Later a new king came to power. He was afraid of the Hebrews because they were strong in number—there were so many, he thought they might try to take over his country. So the

new king made the Hebrews slaves, and they had to work hard for all the kings of Egypt for the next four hundred years.

God knew what was happening, and He rescued His people. (The full story is in Exodus 5–14.) He sent Moses to tell Pharaoh the king, "Let My people go." But Pharaoh said, "No, they can't go." Ten different times, Pharaoh said no! He thought he was stronger than God and could keep the Hebrews as his slaves. But no one is stronger than God—and He saves His people.

God brought His people out slavery and into a good land. He had another rescue planned in the future too—saving us from sin! Ever since Adam and Eve had disobeyed God in the garden, all people everywhere sinned and couldn't stop. God wanted to rescue them. At the right time, God sent Jesus. Because Jesus died and rose again, God saved us from sin like He saved the Hebrews from slavery!

Do you need to be saved or rescued today? Ask God to help you and save you—He will!

Dear God, thank You for Your strong, saving power! I will call out to You. Amen.

- In what ways are you strong? In what ways is God strong?
- Have you ever been in trouble and had someone help or rescue you?

GO DEEPER

When trouble comes and you need to be rescued, what should you do? Psalm 18:3 will tell you.

Saved to Do Good

In Christ Jesus, God made us new people
so that we would do good works.

Ephesians 2:10 ICB

Eleven-year-old Ethan Woody wanted to give every homeless person in his town a warm blanket for Christmas. Ethan and his mom invited people to donate. They collected 118 blankets, dozens of pairs of socks, and enough items like soap and toothpaste to fill several boxes. Ethan wanted the people who received the gifts to know that "Somebody out there cares."

Christians all over the world do good works to help people and share God's love. Some build hospitals, schools, and churches in places that don't have them. Some take care of orphans. Others teach farmers how to grow better crops to feed their families. Some teach reading to grown-ups who never learned how. Some gather eyeglasses and shoes for children who need them, and others take a meal to a sick neighbor or walk that neighbor's dog.

Children can do good works too! Ethan certainly did. Other children have sold lemonade or crafts and donated their earnings to help find a cure for cancer. Visiting with people at a retirement home or putting on a play for them are other ways to do good, and you can ask God to help you discover many more. God saved us not only to do good works, but the rest of Ephesians 2:10 tells us that God planned in advance what those good works would be!

When we do good works in Jesus' name, people feel God's love for them. What good works can you do to show others that God loves them and wants to save them too?

Dear God, thank You for sending Jesus to save me. Show me the ways I can do good works for others, now and as I grow up. Amen.

- What is the best thing you've ever done for someone else?
- What do you think it means to do good works in Jesus' name?

GO DEEPER

A famous Bible verse we call the Golden Rule tells us one way to do good for others. Read Luke 6:31.

THE LORD WILL PROVIDE
Jehovah Jireh (jeh-HO-vuh *JYE*-ruh)

Miracle Bread

So Abraham called the name of that place, "The LORD will provide."

Genesis 22:14

The chorus of a well-known hymn goes like this: "Count your blessings, name them one by one. Count your blessings, see what God has done!"

Have you ever tried to count all your blessings? The list would be long, because *everything* you have is a gift from God! Air to breathe, food to eat, clothes to wear, a place to live, a beautiful world to see, music to hear, and people who love you. The Bible says God "richly provides us with everything to enjoy" (1 Timothy 6:17).

God knows what we need and provides it for us. Everyone gets hungry, right? After Moses led God's people out of Egypt, what would they eat? God sent them manna to gather and eat during all the years they lived in the wilderness. The manna tasted like wafers made with honey, and the people could bake bread and make hot cereal with it too. [Read the full story in Exodus 16.]

The Israelites didn't need to worry. God had already shown them He could take care of them. We don't need to worry either. "Pray and ask God for everything you need. And when you pray, always give thanks" (Philippians 4:6 ICB).

And did you know that God sometimes uses *us* to provide what others need? When homes are damaged in a flood, people help one another clean up. We can collect supplies for a food drive, help serve meals at homeless shelters, or start a lemonade stand to collect money for missionaries. In fact, one reason God blesses us is so we can be a blessing to others! How could you be a blessing to someone else today?

Dear God, thank You for knowing what I need and being my Jehovah Jireh, The Lord Will Provide. Help me use my blessings to bless others too. Amen.

• Name at least ten things God has provided for you.
• How could you bless someone in need this week?

GO DEEPER

How does God care for the earth so it will provide food for us? Read Psalm 65:9–13.

In Our Place

*Abraham answered, "God will give us
the lamb for the sacrifice, my son."*

Genesis 22:8 ICB

Remember Abraham? He waited a *long* time for the son God had promised. And even before Isaac was born, Abraham loved him mightily! But Abraham loved God even more.

When Isaac was a boy, God tested Abraham. (You can read the full story in Genesis 22.) He sent Abraham into the mountains to offer Isaac as a sacrifice. Abraham trusted God and was determined to obey Him, but he also believed God would provide a way out. At just the right time, Abraham saw a lamb nearby, caught in a bush. God had provided the lamb for the sacrifice in Isaac's place!

Many years later, God provided another sacrifice: Jesus. God wants His children to live with Him forever, but there was a problem—our sin. God solved that problem by sending Jesus to take the punishment for sin on the cross, even though Jesus had never done one thing wrong.

Jesus died on the cross as a sacrifice for our sin. But each of us needs to choose to believe—to trust—that Jesus died for us.

Angels rejoice whenever anyone decides to turn from sin and follow Jesus! Are you ready for Jesus to be your Savior? Believe that Jesus is God's Son and that He died for you. Talk with a parent, older friend, or church leader. Be baptized. Keep learning

more from God's Word, the Bible, every day. Be glad for how God provides for you!

Dear God, thank You for providing a way for me to live with You forever. Thank You for giving us Jesus. I want to follow Him! Amen.

- Why do you think God wanted to provide a sacrifice for our sin?
- Who is Jesus to you?

GO DEEPER

Does God love us only when we're good? Find the answer in Romans 5:8.

Perfectly Perfect

God, the Holy One, says, "Can you
compare me to anyone?"

Isaiah 40:25 ICB

In the dark movie theater, you tripped and spilled your popcorn. You've been practicing every day, but you still can't memorize your piano piece. You tried out for cheerleading, but you didn't make the squad. You wanted to do the right thing, but you did something wrong instead. Guess what? No matter how hard you try, you'll never be perfect! None of us can be perfect here on earth.

Only God, the Holy One, is perfect. God is perfect and good in every way. He is different from us. He can do anything. *Holy* means "set apart." There's no person or power higher or better than God. But even though He is perfect and we are not, God still loves us and wants to be with us!

God told Moses how to build a beautiful worship tent, the tabernacle. (You can read more about this in Exodus 35–40.) It would remind God's people that He is holy, and it would be a place where God could be right there with them as they camped and traveled toward the Promised Land. To make the tabernacle, the people gave gifts: gold, silver, and bronze; thread colored red, purple, and blue; linen and leather; acacia wood and jewels; olive oil and spices. Their gifts pleased God because the people gave them gladly.

The gifts we give gladly please God too! Did you get money for your birthday? Can you sing or play an instrument? Are you good at sports or writing or art? What possession, talent, or ability could you give or use to tell others about God's wonderful love? You don't have to be perfect—only God is perfect. Just give what you can with a happy and grateful heart.

Dear God, thank You for loving me even though I'm not perfect and You are. Show me how to give gifts to worship You and tell others about Your holy, perfect love. Amen.

- Have you ever wanted to give up an activity because you couldn't do it perfectly? What happened?
- Why do we sometimes think we have to be perfect for God to love us?

GO DEEPER

What kind of giver does God love to see? Find out in 2 Corinthians 9:7.

Part of the Family

*How very much our Father loves us, for he calls
us his children, and that is what we are!*

1 John 3:1 NLT

When Kristen Brozina was in fourth grade, she and her dad began a challenge they called "The Streak." Kristen's dad read aloud to her 3,218 nights in a row, until she went to college! The Streak became a special tradition of their family.

Maybe your family always goes together to find a Christmas tree, or eats pancakes every Saturday morning, or sings in the car on family vacations. Probably everyone in your family works and does chores. The people in a family care for one another and spend time working and playing together. Everyone has a special place in the family.

It's the same in God's family too! At Mount Sinai, God promised the Israelites He would care for them as His treasured people if they would trust Him and obey His laws. Later on, God made a new promise to all people—He will adopt us as His children if we love and trust His Son, Jesus, who died on the cross for our sins and then was raised to life.

When God, the Holy One, saves us and adds us to His family, we begin to live holy lives too. We each have a special place in God's family, with privileges and responsibilities including these:

- Our sins are forgiven.
- We can worship and praise God.
- We can talk to God anytime about anything, and He will hear us.
- We can ask God for what we need, and He will take care of us.
- We do good works to help others in need.
- We know that someday we will live with God in heaven.
- We tell others about Jesus and how they can become God's children too.

How wonderful that God, the Holy One, loves us and wants us to be His children forever!

Dear God, thank You that I can be Your child forever. Thank You for making me part of Your family. Amen.

- What do you like about your family?
- What do you like about being part of God's family?

GO DEEPER

What is God's family called today? Discover the answer in Acts 20:28.

Follow Directions

Moses built an altar and called the name of it, The LORD Is My Banner.

Exodus 17:15

In the United States, June 14 is Flag Day. On June 14 in 1777, the stars-and-stripes design was approved as the first official American flag—the "star-spangled banner." Wherever the flag is seen—over schools, stadiums, government buildings, and homes—it means the people there love and honor the United States of America and follow its laws.

Some churches have a Christian flag or banners for different seasons of the church year. But even without an actual flag, banner, or sign, all Christians have a way to show that God is the One we love and honor.

How? By what we do. At the battle of Jericho, Joshua and the Israelite army followed God's directions. (You can read the story in Joshua 6.) They marched around the city walls once a day for six days and seven times on the seventh day—without saying a word. The only sounds were their footsteps and the priests blowing trumpets. On the seventh day, after the army marched around the city seven times, Joshua yelled, "Shout!" and everyone did!

What a strange way to fight a battle! The soldiers might have felt a little silly. But they wanted to love and honor God—The Lord My Banner—so they trusted Him and followed His directions. And the walls of Jericho fell down.

In the Bible, we have directions from God that teach us right and wrong. Sometimes we want to do the right thing, but we do the wrong thing to please other kids or fit in with friends. (We call that peer pressure.) When you feel peer pressure, stop and think, and let The Lord My Banner lead you. Follow His directions instead. Like Joshua and the army at Jericho, you'll be glad you did!

> Dear God, You are the One I want to follow. I love You, God. I will trust You to lead me every day. Amen.

• When have you felt peer pressure to do the wrong thing?
• Are God's directions easy or hard to follow?

GO DEEPER

What did King David write about trusting God to lead him? Find out in Psalm 23:3.

Have a Good Day

His banner over me is love.

Song of Solomon 2:4 ICB

Ever had a bad day? Maybe you forgot your homework or struck out at softball practice. Maybe you are worried about someone who is sick or a big test coming up. Everyone experiences troubles and problems, but God always loves us and leads us through the hard times.

Not long after the Israelites left Egypt, a group of people called the Amalekites began a fight with them. (You can find this story in Exodus 17:8–16.) In Bible times, armies carried flags or banners into battle. On the second day of the battle, Moses stood on a hill and held up his staff as a banner, or sign, that God's people were trusting His power to help them.

As long as Moses held up his staff, the Israelites were winning the battle. But when Moses' arms got tired and he put his arms down, the Israelites began to lose. So Moses' brother Aaron and his friend Hur found a big stone for Moses to sit on. Then they stood on either side of him and held up his arms so Moses could hold up his staff! After the Israelites won the battle, Moses built an altar and called it "The Lord My Banner." God loved His people and had used His power to help them.

When you have a problem, you can always trust God to lead you through it. His banner over you is love. That means He will show His love for you, as proud as a flag flying in front of an army as they march out to battle. Even if you don't understand what is happening or why, you can still trust and follow God. God will provide you with help and a solution, just like he did for Moses. What problem will you trust Him with today?

Dear God, thank You for Your power and love that lead and protect me like a banner. Amen.

- Have you ever had a really bad day? What happened?
- How has God helped you with a problem in the past?

GO DEEPER

We often don't know how to solve a problem, but God knows. Read Ephesians 3:20.

51

Peace with God

*Then Gideon built an altar there to the
LORD and called it, The LORD Is Peace."*

Judges 6:24

When you were younger, were you afraid of the dark? Maybe at night you worried about monsters. You thought they were real and would pop out to "get you."

Some people think about God like that. They think He's always waiting for them to do something wrong so He can punish them. But that's not what God is like!

God sent an angel to tell Gideon that God had chosen him to save His people from their enemies. (You can read the whole story in Judges 6–7.) The angel called Gideon "mighty warrior," but Gideon felt small and weak. How could he lead God's people? The angel said, "God will be with you." Gideon felt afraid of God, but God said, "Don't worry, Gideon. Be at peace."

What's *peace*? Feeling good. Feeling complete and unafraid because God is with you. Being who God made you to be, and not trying to be what someone else says you should be. (Satan wants us to believe God doesn't care about us. But Satan lies, remember?)

Gideon obeyed God and followed His instructions. Armed only with torches and trumpets—no weapons—Gideon and just three hundred men surprised and scared their enemies at night, and they all ran away without a fight.

Gideon learned God was *for* him and all His people. God didn't want them living in fear of anyone. He wanted them to trust Him and live in peace. God wants the same for you. He is *always* for you and wants what's best for you. You can have peace because God is with you, and you never have to be afraid of Him!

Dear God, thank You for giving me peace.
Help me always trust You! Amen.

• Have you ever felt afraid of God? When?
• What are some ways God shows you He is for you?

GO DEEPER

What did the angels say about peace on the night Jesus was born? Look in Luke 2:14.

Blessed Are the Peacemakers

*"Blessed are the peacemakers: for they
shall be called the children of God."*

Matthew 5:9 KJV

In December 1982, ten-year-old Samantha Smith wrote a letter to the new leader of the Soviet Union. She asked him what he was doing to keep from having a war. A few months later, she got a letter back with an invitation to visit Russia with her family that summer. The Soviet people loved seeing this young American girl, and Samantha became known as America's youngest ambassador for peace.

Samantha was a *peacemaker*. She did what she could to help two countries live together without fighting. In her letter, Samantha said, "God made the world for us to live together in peace."

Jesus said peacemakers would be called God's children. Why? Because God is a peacemaker too! The Bible tells us, "We have peace with God because of what Jesus Christ our Lord has done for us" (Romans 5:1 NLT). God sent Jesus to take the punishment for our sin so we could be forgiven and have a forever life with Him. That's good news! We call this good news the *gospel*.

You can be a peacemaker too. If you take a friend to VBS, or give your allowance for a special offering, or share the gospel with someone, you're being a peacemaker. Living in peace with others is being a peacemaker too. You can decide not to fight with someone even if you know you are right, for example, and you can stay calm when things go wrong or when you feel angry.

Children often look like and act like their parents do. So since God is called The Lord Is Peace, it just makes sense His kids would be peacemakers too! How will you be a peacemaker today?

Dear God, I want everyone to know Jesus and have peace. Please help me be a peacemaker. Amen.

- When have you been a peacemaker? What happened?
- How can we have peace with God?

GO DEEPER

Is it always possible to have peace with others? What does Romans 12:18 say?

Be Comforted

*Blessed be the God and Father of our Lord Jesus
Christ, the Father of mercies and God of all comfort.*

2 Corinthians 1:3

Losing something or someone important never feels good.
Whether we've lost a pet, didn't place in a race, or moved far
away from our best friend, losing hurts.

Ruth and her mother-in-law, Naomi, came to Bethlehem
feeling hurt and sad. (You can read their whole story in the book
of Ruth.) Naomi's husband and sons had died. Ruth had been
married to one of Naomi's sons, so now she was alone too.
But together Ruth and Naomi trusted God, and He comforted
them by taking care of them every day and giving them a happy
new life.

And that's not all. After Ruth met and married a kind man named Boaz, they had a baby, Obed. He grew up to be the grandfather of Israel's King David, and many years later, Jesus was born from David's family. So Ruth, a foreigner who had lost everything, became an ancestor of Jesus, the Son of God, who gives us everything and came to save and comfort us. What a story!

God cares about us. He cares about you! He watches over our lives and comforts us in our troubles. He might send a friend to give you a hug. He might put a beautiful sunset in the sky to remind you you're never alone. He can even turn your troubles, or anything you've lost, into something good, as He did for Ruth and Naomi. "We know that in everything God works for the good of those who love him" (Romans 8:28 ICB).

So if you feel hurt or sad today, keep your eyes open for how God will comfort you. You just might be surprised!

> Dear God, thank You for knowing me
> so well and comforting me when I
> am hurt or sad. I love You. Amen.

- What have you lost that was important to you?
- Why do you think God wants to comfort us?

GO DEEPER

Is there any situation too bad for God to comfort us? Look in 2 Corinthians 1:4 to find out.

Pass It On

He comforts us every time we have trouble, so that
we can comfort others when they have trouble.

2 Corinthians 1:4 ICB

Nine-year-old Mason Hymer wanted to do something to give hope to kids going into foster care. He remembered being a scared, lonely three-year-old, riding in a car with a social worker to what would be his new home. He had nothing with him except the clothes he was wearing.

Mason thought about what would have comforted him on that drive. With his sister, MacKenzie, he created Bundles of Hope to give a backpack with pajamas, toothpaste and a toothbrush, and a stuffed animal to children headed to foster families. More than a thousand children have received the bundles—including two of Mason and MacKenzie's now-adopted siblings, who arrived at the Hymer home carrying their bundles.

Mason had found the comfort of a good foster home and being adopted, and his experiences showed him how he could comfort other kids new to foster care. Mason and MacKenzie include a handmade tag on every bundle that says, "There is surely a future hope for you, and your hope will not be cut off" (Proverbs 23:18 NIV).

God often works like that. He comforts us when we are sad or in need, and then we know how to comfort others. And when we do, we show them God cares about them and loves them too. Knowing God loves us and sent Jesus to be our Savior is the very best comfort of all!

So look around you at school, at church, on the field, or on your street. Do you see someone who is hurting or sad? Offer a smile or a helping hand. Remember how God has comforted you, and pass it on.

Dear God, thank You for caring about Your children and comforting us. Help me pass on Your love and comfort to others. Amen.

• How has someone comforted you?
• What could you do to comfort someone else?

GO DEEPER

When God's people were in trouble, what message from God did the prophet Jeremiah give them? Read Jeremiah 31:13.

Open to All

Much comfort comes to us through Christ.

2 Corinthians 1:5 ICB

Imagine moving to a new country where everything is unfamiliar. The people speak a language you don't understand, they eat new foods with strange names, and they celebrate holidays you've never heard of. Their hair and skin color and clothing might be very different from yours too. Yikes—making a move like that could be really challenging!

When Ruth came to Bethlehem with Naomi, she was a foreigner, an outsider. How would she be treated? Ruth counted on God to help her. She told Naomi, "Every place you go, I will go. . . . Your people will be my people. Your God will be my God." (Ruth 1:16 ICB).

The workers in the wheat and barley fields treated Ruth kindly. They left grain for her to pick up and take home to make bread for Naomi and Ruth to eat. They spoke well of Ruth and told the field's owner, Boaz, how hard she worked. The village people talked about how kindly Ruth cared for Naomi. Before long, Boaz and Ruth married. And that's how Ruth, a foreigner, became part of the family that brought Jesus, the Savior, into the world many years later!

When God gave the apostle John a vision of heaven, John saw "so many people that no one could count them. They were from every nation, tribe, people, and language of the earth"

[Revelation 7:9 ICB]. Every person from every place is important to God! And so they must be important to us too.

How do we treat others who are different from us? Who come from other places? It matters to God! How could you be a comforting friend to someone different from you today?

Dear God, help me be a friend to everyone, and especially to those who are different from me. Everyone matters to You! Amen.

- What are some of the ways people are different from one another?
- What are some of the ways all people are alike?

GO DEEPER

Does God think some people are more important than others? Read Acts 10:34.

All Fall Down

The LORD, whose very name is Jealous, is a God
who is jealous about his relationship with you.

Exodus 34:14 NLT

Wherever the Israelites lived, the people of the nations around them worshiped and prayed to other gods. Those gods weren't real, but people believed in them and made statues and objects of stone, precious metals, or wood—idols—to represent them.

Wow! Instead of worshiping the Creator—our powerful God who made the world and everything in it—people worshiped objects they made themselves that had *no* power at all! The Philistines, for example, worshiped a god they called Dagon, and they had a statue of him in their temple. But when they placed the Ark of the Covenant (which came from God's tabernacle) next to that statue, what happened? The idol fell over—twice—and its head and hands broke off. (You can read this story in 1 Samuel 5.)

God told the Israelites never to worship idols. He was *jealous* for His people. He wanted what was best for them—a forever relationship with Him. Sometimes, though, the Israelites *did* worship idols. They wanted to be like the people all around them more than they wanted to obey and worship God.

God is jealous for us too! He is the only One who can care for us because He made us and He saves us. God is the only One we should worship. But anything we think is better or more important than God can become an idol to us—sports, clothes, games, grades, or caring more about what our friends think than what God thinks, for example.

What's most important to you? Do you have any idols in your life? Remember that our Jealous God wants what's best for you, and let Him be the only One you worship.

Dear God, I'm glad You want what's best for me! Help me put You first and obey and worship only You. Amen.

- God is jealous in a good way. There's also a bad kind of jealousy. Can you describe it?
- How do you think something in our lives becomes an idol?

GO DEEPER

Read Jeremiah 10:1–5 for a funny—but serious—description of idols.

All the Children of the World

"God loved the world so much
that he gave his only Son."

John 3:16 ICB

Do you remember singing this little song when you were younger? "Jesus loves the little children, all the children of the world . . ." It's true—Jesus does love *all* the children of the world. But some children don't know who Jesus is.

That's because all over the world, and wherever you live, people today still worship and pray to other gods, just like people did in Bible times. You might have friends at school or neighbors on your street who are Muslim, Buddhist, or Hindu, for example. They believe in other gods, not the God of the Bible.

But there's only *one* God. Those other gods aren't real. Jesus said, "I am the way, and the truth, and the life. No one comes to the Father except through me" [John 14:6]. And Jesus proved these words are true by dying on the cross for our sins and then rising again.

So what should you do if you know people who haven't heard this yet or don't believe it?

- First, love them. Because Jesus does!
- *Respect* their beliefs—don't make fun of them. Everyone has a right to believe whatever they would like to.
- Let your light shine for Jesus every day. Be kind. Do good. And if your friends ask you why, tell them about Jesus' love!
- And pray. Ask God to bless your friends and show them the way to follow Him.

Remember, God is jealous for His people—He wants what's best for us, and what's best for everyone is to love and worship Him!

Dear God, You love *all* the people You made and want what's best for them. May everyone hear about Your love and believe in You. Amen.

- What are some reasons your friends and neighbors might not know about Jesus?
- What are some ways to let your light shine for Jesus?

GO DEEPER

Read Psalm 117:1. Someday, this will happen!

Baa, Baa, Baa

The LORD is my shepherd.

Psalm 23:1

If you could be an animal, what would you be? A tall giraffe? A cuddly koala? A bouncy kangaroo? A powerful lion or bear? Maybe not a sheep. But did you know the Bible says people are like sheep?

Before David became king of Israel, he worked as a shepherd. He knew a lot about sheep and a lot about being a shepherd. Sheep need a shepherd, or else they can get into trouble fast.

In Psalm 23, David tells us that God takes care of His people as a shepherd takes care of sheep. (You can find this in the book of Psalms.)

A shepherd takes his sheep where there is good grass to eat and quiet streams of water to drink from. (Sheep don't like noise.) He finds cool, shady places for them to safely rest. He keeps them well with oil on their noses to shoo flies away. At night he builds a fire to scare wild animals nearby. He guides the sheep away from dangerous places and shows them the good paths to follow. He saves them when they wander and get lost. The sheep aren't afraid of anything because the shepherd uses his strength and his staff to protect and comfort them.

Sheep have everything they need if they have a good shepherd. And we have everything we need because God is Jehovah Roi, The Lord My Shepherd. Does God provide the things we need? Does He guide us and show us what is right and what is wrong? Does He keep us safe and comfort us? Does He search for the people who wander away from Him? Does He save them? Oh, yes!

How is God caring for you as your Shepherd today?

Dear God, I'm so glad to be one of Your sheep. Thank You for being my shepherd! Amen.

- How do people wander away from God and get lost?
- How does God save lost people?

GO DEEPER

Read another verse about sheep and the Shepherd. Read Psalm 100:3.

An Unlikely Choice

*"A good person has good things saved up in his heart.
And so he brings good things out of his heart."*

Luke 6:45 ICB

Have you ever picked up a book with an ugly cover that turned out to be a story you loved? Or a book with an exciting cover that turned out to be a big disappointment? We can't always tell what's on the inside just by looking at the outside!

The prophet Samuel thought for sure that God would choose Jesse's oldest son, Eliab—who was tall and handsome—to be the next king of Israel. But Samuel was wrong.

Jesse had left his youngest son, David, in the fields, tending sheep. Maybe Jesse thought David was too young and or not smart enough to be king. But Jesse was wrong too. (You can find this story in 1 Samuel 16.)

Samuel told Jesse to send for David, and when David arrived, God told Samuel, "This is the one. Anoint him."

That's how Samuel learned that God doesn't judge people by how they look on the outside but by what's in their hearts. All people everywhere are valuable to God.

So when we meet people who don't have the best clothes, or who are overweight or skinny, or can't speak clearly or walk well, how should we treat them? And when we meet people who are always in style, or good athletes, or popular and fun to be around, how should we treat them?

The answer is that we should treat them all the same—because none of those on-the-outside things matter. God cares about what's in our hearts. Do we love Him and want to do what's right? That's the most important thing.

Dear God, help me get to know what people are like in their hearts and not judge by how they look on the outside. Amen.

- When is one time you've been surprised by something that turned out to be not what you expected?
- Have you ever not wanted to be friends with others because of how they looked?

GO DEEPER

How can we know what is in someone's heart? Read Luke 6:43–45.

Songs of Praise

He put a new song in my mouth, a
song of praise to our God.

Psalm 40:3

If sheep could talk, what would they say? Maybe "We love our shepherd! He cares for us!" or "Thank you, shepherd, for how you help us!" or "Everyone should praise our wonderful shepherd!"

When he was a young shepherd, Israel's King David played a stringed instrument called a lyre (something like a small harp), and he wrote songs to sing out in the fields with his sheep. Even after he was king, David wrote songs. David knew God always takes care of us like a good shepherd, and he filled his songs with thanks and praise for God's goodness, mercy, power, and love. We can find the words to many of David's songs in the Bible, in the book of Psalms.

David said he would always praise God: "I will praise the Lord at all times. His praise is always on my lips" (Psalm 34:1 ICB). In good times and bad times, praising God puts our thoughts on Him and helps us remember all His promises. Just like sheep need to keep their eyes on the shepherd and listen for his voice, we need to keep God, our Shepherd, in our thoughts and listen to His words. Praising God helps us do that.

Music and singing are good ways to praise God, but they're not the only ways. You can sing a song, write a poem, draw a picture, do a dance, say a Bible verse, give a shout or whisper

a prayer, do a somersault, clap, or be kind to someone in Jesus' name. How could you praise God, your Shepherd, right now?

Dear God, help me praise You every day!
You are my wonderful Shepherd, and
I want to thank You always. Amen.

- Can you think of a time when it's easy to praise God?
- Can you think of a time it might be harder to praise Him?

GO DEEPER

Want to know what it's like to praise the Lord with music? Find Psalm 150 in your Bible, and read it out loud.

Powered by God

The Lord is my strength and shield.
I trust him, and he helps me.

Psalm 28:7 ICB

What does it look like to depend on God's strength?

At the 1924 Olympics, fans thought Eric Liddell had only a small chance of winning the men's four-hundred-meter race, but Eric won *and* broke the world record. Eric wanted his running to honor God, and he depended on God to help him run. He told people, "The secret of my success over the four-hundred-meter is that I run the first two hundred meters as fast as I can. Then, for the second two hundred meters, with God's help I run faster." Eric depended on God to give him strength to run.

David had the same attitude when he fought Goliath. (You can find this story in 1 Samuel 17.) David knew that God would help him win, even though the entire army and even King Saul were afraid of the giant Philistine. Just like David depended on God's strength when he rescued his sheep from lions and bears, David depended on God to help him defeat Goliath.

For Eric Liddell and for David, depending on God also looked like not trying to be something they weren't. Eric wouldn't race on a Sunday—he didn't believe that was right. David wouldn't wear King Saul's heavy armor—he wasn't used to it, and it would have slowed him down.

You might not fight against giants or run in the Olympics. But you might have to take a hard test. You might have to deal with a bully. You might have to say no to friends who want you to disobey your parents.

How will it look for *you* to depend on God?

Dear God, be my strength when I have to do hard things. I want to depend on You. Amen.

- What is the hardest thing you've ever had to do?
- Do you think David worried about fighting Goliath? Why or why not?

GO DEEPER

What should you do when you need God's strength? Psalm 138:3 will tell you.

Only a Boy Named David

*I will trust, and will not be afraid; for
the LORD GOD is my strength.*

Isaiah 12:2

Have you ever received an award—maybe a trophy or a ribbon in a sports competition, an art contest, or a spelling bee? Awards honor people for what they have accomplished. No one gets an award every day. But God deserves our honor all the time, and He will give us the strength to stand up for Him even when it's hard.

David heard Goliath making fun of God, and no one in the army would defend God's name. David's brothers, the rest of the Israelite army, and even King Saul laughed at David because David said he would fight Goliath. But with God's strength to help him, David fought the giant—and won.

You will probably never have to fight a giant, but you can honor God's name as David did. Whenever you have an opportunity, speak up. Don't be afraid. Show up at See You at the Pole to pray. Join that Christian club. Talk about the Christian movies you see. Do what's right because you follow God: Tell your friends you won't join in gossip with them, and walk away. Reach out to the lonely kids at school or church. Study for the big test and say no to anyone who wants you to help them cheat. And pray that all who see you will know that you depend on the power you get from God, The Lord My Strength.

Dear God, even though I'm young, I want to depend on Your strength and honor You like David did. Be my strength always. Amen.

- What awards do you know about? How do you think it feels to be honored with an award?
- What are some opportunities for you to take a stand for God?

GO DEEPER

When you face any challenge, what should you remember? Read Isaiah 41:10.

How to See in the Dark

The LORD is my light.

Psalm 27:1

In the dark, it's good to have a guide with a light. An usher with a flashlight helps us find our seats in a dark theater. The moon shines on the path for our nighttime hike. A lighthouse guides ships away from the shore. Without light, we can easily stumble or get lost. And just as light guides us in the dark, wisdom guides us in life.

King Solomon knew he would need wisdom to be a good king. He would need to know how to make good decisions. So when God came to him in a dream and offered to give him anything he asked for, Solomon asked for wisdom: "Lord my God, you have allowed me to be king in my father's place. But I am like a little child. I do not have the wisdom I need to do what I must do. . . . So I ask that you give me wisdom. Then I can rule the people in the right way. Then I will know the difference between right and wrong" [1 Kings 3:7, 9 ICB]. [You can read the whole story in 1 Kings 3:1–15.]

Solomon's request for wisdom pleased God. Solomon became known as the wisest man in the world, and people came from all over to listen to him.

We all need wisdom for the choices we make every day. Will you obey your parents, or do something they've told you not to do? Will you help your elderly neighbor trying to get across the street, or pretend you didn't see she needed help? Will you honor God with your words, or will you use His name carelessly? God has wisdom for you to answer all these questions and more!

Be like Solomon. Ask God for wisdom. Depend on The Lord My Light to be your guide. Follow His wise ways like light in the dark, and you will have a good and joyful life.

Dear God, I need Your wisdom every day. Help me learn. Teach me what I need to know, and help me do it. Amen.

• What is the darkest place you have ever been?
• Is there a problem you need wisdom for right now?

GO DEEPER

Where is an important place for finding God's wisdom and light? Read Psalm 119:105.

What Flavor?

The path of the righteous is like the light of dawn,
which shines brighter and brighter until full day.

Proverbs 4:18

Do you like ice cream? At an ice cream shop, how do you decide what to get? You can choose from so many flavors, like cookies and cream, chocolate chip cookie dough, mini peanut butter cup, and birthday cake. It can be hard to make a decision!

You probably don't eat ice cream every day, but every day *can* bring something to decide about. Will you study for the big test, or cheat? Will you be kind to the kids with disabilities, or make fun of them? Will you read your Bible, or watch TV?

When you have decisions to make, it's important to choose carefully which light you want shining on your path to help you— the wisdom of the world or the wisdom of God. So what's the difference?

Worldly wisdom says what *you* want is always best, but God's wisdom says *His* ways are best: "The wisdom that comes from God is like this: First, it is pure. Then it is also peaceful, gentle, and easy to please. This wisdom is always ready to help those who are troubled and to do good for others. This wisdom is always fair and honest" [James 3:17 ICB].

When Solomon became king and started to rule God's people, he asked The Lord My Light for wisdom, and he pleased God with his choice. You can please God too, when you choose His wisdom. Not sure how to get it? The Bible is full of God's wisdom! And when you have to make a decision in life, "if you need wisdom, ask our generous God, and he will give it to you" [James 1:5 NLT].

Dear God, I want to choose Your wisdom and have Your light shining on my path every day. Please help me make the right choices! Amen.

- What are some examples of worldly wisdom?
- When might you need God's wisdom to help you make a decision?

GO DEEPER

Where does godly wisdom begin? Look in Psalm 111:10 to find out.

Love to Learn

Every good gift and every perfect gift is from above.
James 1:17

Babies learn new things every day, and they never stop learning. Curious babies and toddlers want to know all about the world around them, and they love to explore. This is how God made them—and us! We should keep growing and love learning new things all our lives.

Sometimes it's hard. Maybe you love learning about science but have trouble with geography or history. Maybe other kids learn new things faster than you. That's okay! We are all different. Just keep on learning! The Bible says, "God . . . made the world and everything in it" (Acts 17:24). He filled the world with wonderful things for us to learn every day and every year of our lives.

Wise King Solomon wanted to understand as much as he could. He studied plants, trees, animals, and fish, and he taught others what he learned. He liked to write—and he left us thousands of songs and wise sayings called proverbs. He supervised the building of the temple and his palace.

God gave you an amazing body with an amazing brain! So use it. Don't zone out staring at a screen for hours at a time. Get outdoors. Play. Discover God's wonders in nature. Try a new sport or a new hobby. Learn about things that interest you, and try your best in your harder subjects.

God promises He will guide you with His light as you explore life and think about what you want to do when you grow up. He may even make a few "light bulbs" come on in your head as you learn! Psalm 37:23 says, "The LORD directs the steps of the godly. He delights in every detail of their lives" [NLT]. Thank God for His gifts to you, and go out and start learning!

Dear God, thank You for making me so I can learn and for the wonderful world to learn about. Amen.

- What do you enjoy learning about the most?
- What would you like to learn more about in the future?

GO DEEPER

Can we ever know as much as God? Read Isaiah 55:8.

Wonderfully Made

"I am the LORD who heals you."

Exodus 15:26 NLT

Our bodies are incredible! Did you know that:

- Your heart beats more than 100,000 times every day?
- Your ears pick up sound but it's really your brain that hears it?
- A baby has about 300 bones, but an adult only 206? (Some join together as the baby grows.)

King David wrote, "I praise you because you made me in an amazing and wonderful way" (Psalm 139:14 ICB). Who made us? God did—Elohim, the Creator. He knows everything about how our bodies work. New skin grows where you get a cut. Your blood fights bad germs that could make you sick. Many times our bodies heal themselves because that's how God made us!

God will help us do the things that keep our bodies healthy too, like choosing good foods to eat, getting lots of exercise, washing our hands, and brushing our teeth well (instead of rushing!).

God can heal us when something goes wrong too. Sometimes He uses doctors and medicine to help us. In the Bible we can read about people God healed to show His power and His love. The story of Naaman in the Old Testament is just one example of God's healing power at work—God healed his skin disease. (You can read Naaman's story in 2 Kings 5:1–14.) Jesus

healed people who were sick, paralyzed, blind, and deaf. After the resurrection, the apostles healed people in Jesus' name too. Even people who are not healed here on earth can look forward to having perfect, healthy bodies forever in heaven.

Every day, you can thank God for being The Lord My Healer by taking care of your body and your health. What new health habit could you begin today?

Dear God, thank You for my amazing body and for healing me when I'm sick. Amen.

- What do you think is most special about how our bodies work?
- What do you do to take care of the body God gave you?

GO DEEPER

We can pray for good health for others too. Read 3 John v. 2.

Take a Dip

Let the one who boasts, boast in the Lord.

2 Corinthians 10:17

Naaman was a VIP—a very important person. He commanded the army in the country of Syria, so he had an important job. And he had an important friend, the king of Syria.

But Naaman had a serious skin disease. When he heard that God had a prophet in Israel who could heal him, he decided to travel to Israel. He took servants and horses and chariots and a letter from his friend, the king of Syria, to the king of Israel.

At Elisha's house, Naaman expected to see the prophet face-to-face, but Elisha didn't even come outside. Instead, he sent out a messenger to tell Naaman, "Go to the Jordan River and wash in it seven times. Then you will be cured of your skin disease."

"The muddy Jordan River?" Naaman argued. Namaan didn't feel so important now, and he didn't like the feeling. He started to go home. But he wanted to be well, so finally he did what Elisha said and obeyed God's instructions. He dipped down into the muddy Jordan River seven times, and after the seventh time, his skin became smooth and clear, like a baby's skin. God had healed him!

Namaan learned some big lessons—he wasn't as important as he had thought, but he was important to God, and God deserved his honor and praise. It's never a good idea to brag about how important we are, but it's always a good idea to tell people about how wonderful God is!

Dear God, thank You for Your healing power! I want to tell others about the wonderful things You do. Amen.

- When have you been tempted to brag about yourself?
- Why do you think every person is important to God?

GO DEEPER

After a lame man was healed by the apostle Peter, what did he do? Look in Acts 3:8 to find out.

No More Sickness, No More Pain

We are healed because of his wounds.

Isaiah 53:5 ICB

If someone you love is sick or hurt and doesn't get better, you wonder why God hasn't healed that person. It *is* hard to understand, isn't it? But here is what we know:

- God loves us.
- God uses bad things to make good things happen.
- If we love Jesus, we go to be with Him forever when our lives on earth end.
- In heaven, everyone is healed!

Because of sin, things go wrong in our world. But God has promised that one day everyone who loves Him will be healed and will live forever with Him. The apostle John saw a vision of heaven. He said, "Now God's home is with men. He will live with them, and they will be his people. God himself will be with them and will be their God. He will wipe away every tear from their eyes. There will be no more death, sadness, crying, or pain" (Revelation 21:3–4 ICB).

And here is something wonderful and amazing: God not only heals our bodies; He also heals our hearts. Our hearts get hurt by our own sins and the sins of others. But God is our healer. He sent Jesus to take the punishment so He could heal us by forgiving all our sins. When God forgives us, He heals our hearts.

Remember, God is the God of Truth and God All-Powerful. He never lies, and He has power to keep every promise. And He promises He is The Lord Who Heals—on earth and in heaven. So believe God's promise, ask Jesus to live in your heart and heal it, and you can look forward to heaven!

Dear God, thank You for healing my body and my heart! Thank You for Jesus and what He did for me. Amen.

• Why is heaven a place to look forward to?
• What do you think heaven will be like?

GO DEEPER

What does Revelation 22:1–2 tell us about the tree of life?

Have You Ever Seen an Angel?

The LORD of Heaven's Armies—he is the King of glory.

Psalm 24:10 NLT

What's the biggest surprise you ever had? A birthday gift you didn't expect? Winning a close game with your team? Having your mom or dad come home from military service in time for Christmas?

In the Bible, Elisha's servant got the surprise of his life when the Syrian army surrounded the city, looking for Elisha. "What are we going to do?" the servant wailed when he saw the army. (This story is found in 2 Kings 6:8–23).

"Don't be afraid," Elisha said. "Many more are with us than with them." Then he prayed, "Oh LORD, let him see what I can see."

That's when Elisha's servant got his big surprise. He saw an army of angels, horses, and chariots of fire, all sent by God to watch over and protect Elisha from the enemy king. They had been there the whole time!

The Bible says God is The Lord of Heaven's Armies. Heaven is filled with angels, and God commands them all. God sent an angel to earth to tell Mary she would be the mother of Jesus. He sent an angel to protect Daniel in the lions' den.

The angels keep their eyes on God, watching for His instructions and ready to obey. They are very real, even though most of the time we can't see them. The Bible says, "He will command his angels concerning you to guard you in all your ways" [Psalm 91:11].

So the next time you ask God for help, just think—He might send that help in the form of one of the angels from heaven's army!

Dear God, thank You for Your angel army! Thank You for always watching over us and protecting us. Amen.

- Do you know any songs about angels?
- How does it feel to know that God has a whole army of angels to protect you?

GO DEEPER

Only two angels in the Bible have names. Find them in Daniel 10:13 and Luke 1:19.

Angel Q & A

*All the angels are spirits who serve God and are
sent to help those who will receive salvation.*

Hebrews 1:14 ICB

When people in the Bible saw angels, they usually felt afraid. Why is that? We sometimes see pictures of cute, chubby angels or angels with long hair and flowing robes. But are those true pictures? What should we know and remember about angels?

Who made the angels? God did, before the creation of the world.

What do angels look like? The angels of heaven's army are spirits, so they don't have bodies like ours. And most of the time, we don't see the angels. In the Bible, when angels took on a form that could be seen, they nearly always appeared strong, tall, and powerful. Sometimes they looked like ordinary people.

Do angels have wings? Certain angels called cherubim and seraphim have wings, but no other angels in the Bible are described with wings.

What do angels do? We don't know everything they do, but the Bible tells us that:

- Angels bring special messages from God.
- Angels protect and rescue people.
- Angels rolled the stone away from Jesus' tomb and announced that Jesus was alive.
- Angels celebrate whenever someone is saved.
- Angels fight battles in the heavenly places.

Are the angels more important than Jesus? No. Jesus, God's Son, is our Savior.

Does everyone have a guardian angel? All God's angels guard God's people and do whatever He tells them to do.

We can thank God for the angels in heaven's army, but—like the angels—we worship and praise God!

Dear God, I'm glad I can learn about the angels and worship and praise You! Amen.

- What books, movies, or TV shows have angel characters?
- How do those angels match or not match what the Bible tells us about angels?

GO DEEPER

What animal in the Bible saw an angel? Read Numbers 22:23.

It's Not Science Fiction

Even Satan disguises himself as an angel of light.

2 Corinthians 11:14

Sometimes a scary movie makes us laugh because it seems too silly to be true. Other times we might like being scared just a little. We know it's just a movie, not something true. But there *are* powers of evil in the world we need to know about, even though we may never see them.

It's hard to believe, but long ago, one of the angels thought he could take God's place. Other angels joined him in a rebellion against God. Of course, no one is stronger than The Lord of Heaven's Armies, and He rules over all. God threw that angel—Satan (also called the devil)—and the other rebellious angels out of heaven.

Now, since Satan can't win against God, He fights God's people instead. He tries to trick us by making things that are bad for us seem like good things. The Bible says he even "disguises himself as an angel of light." That means he tries to get us to love and follow him instead of God.

One way the devil tries to trick us is with fortune tellers, palm readers, crystal balls, mediums, psychics, Ouija boards, and even some kinds of meditation. God tells us to stay away from these kinds of things, because they are dangerous. He also tells us to worship Him only!

The Bible, God's Word, tells us what is true so we will recognize Satan's lies. But the best protection we have is God Himself, because He is The Lord of Heaven's Armies. God is in charge and rules over everything—the world we can see and the world we can't see. God has a plan for it all and for us. And the devil does *not* win!

Dear God, thank You for telling us what is good for us and what is not. Help me stay away from the things You tell me to avoid. Amen.

- What are your family's rules for the movies you are allowed to watch?
- If someone asked to tell you your fortune, what would you do?

GO DEEPER

What does Romans 16:20 tell us about our enemy Satan?

Our Strong Protector

He is our help and our shield.

Psalm 33:20

If you found a wallet on the sidewalk at school with a lot of money in it, what would you do? You could keep it and take the money, or you could take the wallet to the office, where the owner might look for it. Keeping the money would be the easy thing, but it wouldn't be the right thing.

In the Bible, Daniel did the right thing even though it was hard. (You can read his story in Daniel 6.) King Darius made a law that no one should pray to anyone but him (silly king!). Anyone who did would be thrown into a den of hungry lions. But Daniel always prayed to God, three times every day, in his room. What would he do?

Daniel trusted God to help him, and he kept praying to God, not to the king.

Now when the king found out about it, he realized what a bad law he had made. Daniel was thrown into the den of hungry lions. But the lions didn't eat him because God sent an angel to close the lions' mouths!

Like a shield, God protected Daniel. What's a shield? In Bible times, soldiers carried shields into battle to protect them from swords and arrows. Today, soldiers wear special vests to shield their bodies. Choosing to do the right thing is like a shield too, because following God's ways keeps us close to Him, and He protects us from harm.

So when you have a choice to make between the easy thing and the right thing, choose to follow The Lord My Shield!

Dear God, thank You for protecting me like a shield. Help me always choose to do what You say is right. Amen.

- When have you made a choice to do the right thing even though it was hard?
- How did you feel when you made that choice?

GO DEEPER

How does King David describe God in Psalm 18:30?

The Shield of Faith

Hold up the shield of faith to stop
the fiery arrows of the devil.

Ephesians 6:16 NLT

Surprises can be fun, but nobody likes to have tricks played on them—especially not Satan's tricks, because he wants to get us to stop loving God. So we need to say no whenever the devil tempts us to do something wrong. And we have to be ready!

Soldiers wear armor to protect themselves in battle. God gives us special armor to keep us safe and strong when Satan fights against us. It's not armor you can see, but the Bible describes it like this:

> Fasten truth around your waist like a belt. Put on God's approval as your breastplate. Put on your shoes so that you are ready to spread the Good News that gives peace. In addition to all these, take the Christian faith as your shield. With it you can put out all the flaming arrows of the evil one. Also take salvation as your helmet and God's word as the sword that the Spirit supplies. (Ephesians 6:14–17 GW)

Satan's tricks and temptations are like "flaming arrows" he shoots at us, but God protects us like a soldier's shield when we have faith—when we trust Him and choose to do the right thing. That's why God is called The Lord My Shield.

So each day when you get dressed, if Jesus is your Savior, don't forget to wear your armor and carry the shield of faith everywhere you go! Then from head to toe, you'll always be ready to stand up to Satan's attempts to knock you down.

Dear God, I want to do what You say
is right and not let Satan trick me.
Thank You for Your armor and especially
for being The Lord My Shield. Amen.

- How is the shield of faith important for telling Satan no?
- How can you use God's armor when you are tempted to do something wrong?

GO DEEPER

We all sin sometimes, even though we don't want to. What should we do then? Read 1 John 1:9.

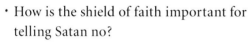

Never Alone

"They shall call his name Immanuel"
(which means, God with us).

Matthew 1:23

Special visitors can be so much fun! Do you have grandparents, aunts and uncles, or cousins who come for visits? When they arrive, you get hugs and high fives because they are so glad to see you. You play games and eat together and take trips to exciting places in your town. But then it's time for the visitors to go back home. You wish they could stay.

When Jesus came to earth as a baby born to Mary, He was a very special visitor. And the best part? This visitor will be with us always! (You can read the story of Jesus' birth in Matthew 1 and Luke 1–2.) Jesus came to rule over God's kingdom forever! Mary's baby was God coming to earth as a human baby, the One God had promised long ago to send—a baby who would be called Immanuel, which means "God with us."

Jesus came to show us what God is like. He came to show us God loves us and wants to be with us forever, here on earth and in heaven. Jesus died on the cross for our sins, but He was raised to life again! He lives forever, and He is here—God With Us—right now and for always.

That means you always have a friend, in good times and bad times, wherever you are, whatever you're doing. You don't ever

have to feel afraid or alone. Jesus is with you to guide you, to teach you, to laugh and cry with you, to love you and forgive you.

Do you need a friend today? Talk to Jesus, who is God With Us.

Dear God, thank You for sending Jesus to show us Your love and to be with us always! Amen.

- When are some times you might feel alone or afraid?
- When have friends helped you? What did they do?

GO DEEPER

Can anything or anyone take God's love away from us? Read Romans 8:38–39.

King in a Stable

He leads the humble in what is right,
and teaches the humble his way.

Psalm 25:9

If you are rich, you can buy anything you want. If you are important, you have bodyguards. And if you are popular, your fans want to take pictures with you wherever you go. Most of us would enjoy being rich, important, or popular, at least for a while. It would be hard for us to give that up. But when Jesus left heaven to come to earth as a baby, He gave up a lot.

Jesus had *everything* He could want—all of heaven's glory! And then He gave it up. God says in the Bible, "He did not think that being equal with God was something to be held on to. He gave up his place with God and made himself nothing. He was born as a man and became like a servant" (Philippians 2:6–7 ICB).

Jesus humbly did what God wanted Him to do. He came as a baby to be the King of God's people. But where was He born? Not in a palace! Jesus was born in a stable, where animals are kept. His bed was an animal's feeding trough filled with hay.

Are there kids you look up to because they are cheerleaders, or get all A's, or play football, or wear cute clothes? Or are *you* someone other kids want to be like? Whenever you start feeling better than others or wanting to be rich, important, or popular, stop. Think about Jesus. He's the King who left glory in heaven to be God With Us. Follow His example and be humble too.

Dear God, help me to be humble like Jesus
and always obey You gladly. Amen.

- What does it mean to be proud? To be humble?
- When have you chosen to be humble instead of bragging about something?

GO DEEPER

When you accomplish a goal, it is okay to be proud of your work, but what else should you be at the same time? Look in Ephesians 5:20.

Why the Angels Sang

God will give a son to us. . . . His name
will be . . . Prince of Peace.

Isaiah 9:6 ICB

Imagine a happy, peaceful scene. Where would you be? At the park with friends? At the beach with your family? Looking up at the moon and stars before you go to bed?

People all around the world want peace. Unfortunately, often there is fighting somewhere in the world. Jesus said, "In this world you will have trouble. But be brave! I have defeated the world!" (John 16:33 ICB). How did Jesus defeat the world? By dying on the cross for sin and being raised to life again.

Fighting goes on in the world because all people sin. Jesus came to defeat sin. He took the punishment for all our sin so God can forgive us! Our sin makes us enemies with God, but because of Jesus we can have peace with God instead.

That's why the angels sang on the night Jesus was born. Angels filled the sky over Bethlehem and said, "Glory to God in the highest, and on earth peace, good will toward men" [Luke 2:14 KJV]. [You can read the whole story in Luke 2:8–20.] The angels sang because God was making peace with us and with all people who would believe in His Son, Jesus.

And when we have peace *with* God, we also can have the peace *of* God—the peace that comes from knowing that no matter what happens, God always loves us and is taking care of us.

Jesus will give His peace to anyone who asks Him. Do you have peace *with* God—is Jesus your Savior? Do you have the peace *of* God—are you trusting Jesus to care for you no matter what happens? You *can* have peace today. Just ask the Prince of Peace!

Dear God, thank You for making a way for us to have peace with You. Thank You for Jesus, the Prince of Peace. Amen.

- When are some times you feel peaceful? When are some times you don't?
- What could you do the next time you feel anxious or worried instead of peaceful?

GO DEEPER

What does Jesus say about peace in John 14:27?

Good News for Everyone

*I bring you good news of great joy
that will be for all the people.*

Luke 2:10

Are there refugees in your community? Kids on your street who don't speak your language? Kids with disabilities at your school? Do you have friends who are different from you in some way, or do you think kids who are different are outsiders?

Do you sometimes feel like an outsider yourself?

The shepherds on the hills near Bethlehem were outsiders. Shepherds got dirty, shaggy, and smelly. They weren't allowed to worship God at the temple like everyone else; they had to stay with their sheep. Shepherds definitely were considered outsiders—people who didn't matter very much.

But that's not what God thought about them! God sent the news about Jesus' birth to the Bethlehem shepherds *first*. Just think, those "outsider" shepherds got to hear the good news about Jesus before anyone else, and they heard it from *angels*!

Some other outsiders heard about Jesus too. They were wise men from the East. When they saw a new star in the sky, they knew it meant the new king of the Jews had been born. They traveled a long, long way to find the baby and worship Him. God had been telling His own people about the coming One for thousands of years, but now was the right time for others to know too.

Everyone matters to God, and everyone needs to know the good news about Jesus.

The next time you feel like an outsider, remember how important you are to God. And the next time *you* think of someone else as an outsider—stop! Remember that the good news about the Prince of Peace is for everyone. Who could you tell about Jesus today?

Dear God, thank You that everyone matters to You. Help me share the good news about Jesus with everyone. Amen.

- Have you ever felt like an outsider? When?
- How could you be a friend to the kids other kids call outsiders?

GO DEEPER

Find one of the places in the Old Testament that tells us about how Jesus would come. Look in Micah 5:2.

Just Like Dad

The child to be born will be called
holy—the Son of God.

Luke 1:35

When you were a baby, people looked at you and said things like "He has his father's eyes" or "She has her mother's nose." And as you grew, you did things that reminded others of your parents too. "He loves to be outside. Takes after his dad!" they said, or "She loves to build things. Might be an engineer like her mom." Children have characteristics of their parents that others can clearly see.

One of Jesus' names in the Bible is Son of God. In Jesus, God came to earth to be with us. Jesus showed us what God is like, the way children resemble their parents.

But Jesus was human like us *and* He was God *at the same time*! He was *holy*—set apart, different. No one else is like Him. He could show us what God is like because He *is* God. (That's why many of the Bible's names for Jesus are the same or similar to the names of God you read about in this book!)

Jesus also was holy because He never sinned. He never did one single thing wrong. He could have, but He didn't. He always did what is right because He is just like His Father.

When we understand who Jesus is, there's only one thing to do—worship and obey Him! How will you worship and obey Jesus, God's Son, today?

Dear God, thank You for Your Son, Jesus. Thank You for sending Him to show us what You are like. I want to obey and worship Jesus every day. Amen.

- What are some ways you look like or act like your parents?
- What are some ways Jesus showed us what God is like?

GO DEEPER

What did the Roman soldier at the cross say about Jesus? Find out in Matthew 27:54.

In My Father's House

*Jesus grew in wisdom and in stature and
in favor with God and all the people.*

Luke 2:52 NLT

Do you sometimes wish you could hurry and grow up? Maybe you're looking forward to being able to stay up later, babysit, get a job, or drive a car. It can be hard to wait until you're older, but growing takes time. That's just how God planned it. Everyone grows from baby to toddler to child to teenager to adult. Even Jesus!

Most of Jesus' growing up took place in a town called Nazareth. His earthly father, Joseph, worked as a carpenter. Jesus learned from Joseph how to build things out of wood. He went to synagogue school to learn to read and memorize Scripture. The Bible says He grew wiser, taller, and stronger and everyone liked Him.

Jesus had to wait until He turned twelve to go with Mary and Joseph to Jerusalem to celebrate the Passover feast and worship God at the temple. (You can read this story in Luke 2:41–52.) When it was time to return to Nazareth, Jesus was still at the temple, talking with the teachers. He was not only asking them questions, but He was answering their questions about God too!

When Mary and Joseph found Jesus talking with the teachers, they were surprised. But Jesus asked, "Why were you looking for me? Didn't you know I needed to be in my Father's house?" Even

though He wasn't grown up yet, Jesus still loved God, learning God's Word, and serving God. Even a child can do that! Even you! You don't have to wait until you grow up. How will you love and serve God today?

Dear God, thank You for Jesus' example. I'm glad I don't have to wait until I'm grown up to know You and serve You! Amen.

- How do you think Jesus treated the other people in Nazareth when He was a child?
- What are some ways you can love and serve God now?

GO DEEPER

What did Jesus say about children and the kingdom of God? Look in Matthew 19:14.

Obey Every Day

Children, always obey your parents,
for this pleases the Lord.

Colossians 3:20 NLT

Do you remember hearing the story of Peter Rabbit when you were younger? Peter disobeyed his mother and went into Mr. MacGregor's garden. Things didn't turn out too well for Peter after that—the farmer chased him all over the garden, and Peter was sick with fright!

Jesus obeyed His parents. When Mary and Joseph found Him in the temple and told Him it was time to go home to Nazareth, He went with them right away and continued to obey their instructions every day. He knew that was the right thing to do and that obedience pleases God.

Parents want what is best for their children, and God has given them the job of helping you grow up to know Him. God doesn't want parents to act harshly, but He does want them to bring up their children "in the discipline and instruction of the Lord" [Ephesians 6:4]. That's the first reason to obey your parents every day.

And here's another reason. Learning to obey your parents when you're a child helps you learn to obey God when you are grown. And obeying God is very important! Jesus, the Son of God, always obeyed His earthly father and His heavenly Father too.

Sometimes you might not be happy with your parents' decisions. Teaching you to follow God's ways sometimes means they have to tell you no or tell you to do something you don't want to do. Do you have trouble obeying your mom or dad? Ask God for His help. Talk to your parents too. Tell them you are sorry for the times you've disobeyed. And then start to follow their instructions and obey every day.

> Dear God, I want to obey my parents, and I want to obey You. Please help me every day! Amen.

- When is it easiest for you to obey your parents?
- When is it hardest for you to obey them?

GO DEEPER

When God gave the Ten Commandments to the Israelites, one rule was about children and parents. Read Exodus 20:12.

Extra! Extra!

*"This is my Son, whom I love—my
Son with whom I am pleased."*

Matthew 3:17 GW

Before the Internet, TV, and radio, people got their news from newspapers. Whenever something big happened, papers printed special editions with all the details. Newsboys stood on city street corners to sell the papers, shouting, "Extra! Extra! Read all about it!"

When God sent His Son, Jesus, to earth, He made sure people knew about it. The shepherds and wise men heard about Jesus when He was a baby. And when Jesus was grown, ready to begin teaching and preaching about God's kingdom, God let people know then too. (You can read this story in Matthew 3.)

First, John the Baptist showed up in the wilderness near the Jordan River. John was Jesus' relative. God had given him the job of announcing, "Prepare the way for the Lord. Make the road straight for him" (Matthew 3:3 ICB). After people confessed their sins, John baptized them.

Then Jesus came to be baptized. John was surprised and tried to stop Him. "Why do You need to be baptized?" John asked, because Jesus had never done anything wrong. "I should be baptized by you instead!" But Jesus answered, "We should do all the things that are right." So John baptized Jesus in the river.

And when Jesus came up out of the water, the Holy Spirit landed on Jesus in the form of a dove. Then God's voice came from heaven, saying, "This is My Son, and I love Him. I am very pleased with Him!"

God's Son has come—the One He promised to send to save His people from their sins. That's news worth shouting about! Do you have friends or neighbors who need to hear all about this good news? Make a plan to tell them very soon!

Dear God, thank You for sending Your Son. Help me to love Him always and to help others know Him and love Him too. Amen.

- Why do you think God said He was pleased with Jesus?
- Can you remember a time you heard some good news or got to tell someone good news? How did you feel?

GO DEEPER

Before Jesus went back to heaven, what did He tell His disciples? Look in Matthew 28:19–20.

Healing Bodies, Healing Souls

"It is the sick who need a doctor. . . . I have come to invite sinners to change their hearts and lives!"

Luke 5:31–32 ICB

Have you ever felt absolutely determined to get something done, no matter what? Maybe it was perfecting a piano piece, getting a good grade on a science project, or raising money for a good cause.

In the Bible, there was a man who couldn't walk, and four of his friends felt absolutely determined to see Jesus so the man could be healed. (This story is found in Luke 5:17–26.)

So when they arrived at the house where Jesus was teaching and couldn't get in because of the crowd . . . and when they got the man on his mat up the stairs to the roof . . . and when they made a hole in the roof big enough to let the man down into the house right in front of Jesus . . . well, Jesus saw how determined the man and his friends were and what great faith they had.

So Jesus told the man, "Friend, your sins are forgiven." But Jesus had authority and power to forgive sins *and* to heal people, and He also said, "Get up, pick up your mat, and go home." And the man did! He walked out the door happy and healed!

We all get sick or hurt sometimes and need healing in our bodies. And we all sin sometimes and need healing in our souls. Jesus has the power to heal bodies and the power to heal souls.

What kind of healing do you need today? Ask Jesus, the Great Physician!

> Dear God, thank You for Jesus, our Great Physician, who can heal bodies and souls. Thank You for Your forgiveness because of what Jesus did on the cross. Amen.

- When have you been sick or hurt and needed healing?
- When have you needed forgiveness?

GO DEEPER

Doctors and medicine are God's gifts to help when we are sick or hurt, but where should our faith be? Read 1 Corinthians 2:5.

Jesus Cares

He had compassion on them and healed their sick.

Matthew 14:14

The 2016 Junior Soccer World Challenge final in Tokyo was a tight 1–0 win for a youth team from Barcelona. Players on the losing team broke into tears. But the Barcelona team had compassion. They consoled their opponents with hugs and told them to hold their heads high. Compassion is understanding how others feel and doing something to help them.

Jesus showed compassion to people who were sick. A man with leprosy came to Jesus and asked to be healed. No one would touch lepers or even go close to them, but what did Jesus do? The Bible tells us: "Moved with compassion, Jesus reached out and touched him. 'I am willing,' he said. 'Be healed!'" (Mark 1:41 NLT).

Jesus is the Great Physician with healing power, but we can pray for people who need healing. We can show kindness— helping our parents take them meals and visiting with them. We can raise money to send medicine to places in the world that don't have enough. We can have compassion like Jesus did!

Jesus cares *a lot* about people in trouble—people who need food or clothing, people in prison, people who are sick. In fact, Jesus said that when we have compassion and help others, it is just as if we were helping Him!

Ask Jesus, the Great Physician, how you can show His love and compassion to others today. How could you help?

Dear God, thank You for Your love and compassion for everyone who needs healing, and thank You for the healing power of Jesus, the Great Physician. Amen.

- How could you help someone near you who is sick or hurting?
- How could you help others in need in other parts of the world?

GO DEEPER

In Luke 17:11–16, how many men with leprosy did Jesus heal? Did they all thank Him?

Shine Your Light

*They said to him, "Rabbi" (which means
Teacher), "where are you staying?"*

John 1:38

Are there people you love to listen to? Maybe storytellers, singers, or favorite teachers or coaches. Maybe your mom or dad reading bedtime stories and praying with you. You love to hear their voices and the things they say.

When Jesus walked through towns and villages, crowds of people gathered to hear what He had to say. They often sat for hours, listening and learning from His teaching. The people had other teachers too, but they knew there was something special about Jesus. He spoke with knowledge and confidence the other teachers didn't have.

The Bible tells us about one special teaching time we call the Sermon on the Mount. (You can find this in Matthew 5–7 and Luke 6:17–49.] So many people had come to hear Jesus that He went up on a mountainside to talk to the people spread out below. The first thing He talked about was the kingdom of God, which means anywhere people let God lead in their hearts. "God blesses you when you depend on Him," He said, "and when you want what is right and good. So be kind and forgiving, and always follow God."

People who live in God's kingdom are like shining lights in the world. "Let your light shine so others can see it," Jesus said. "Don't hide your light. Shine it around so others can find God and follow Him too."

Just like the people on the mountainside, we can follow Jesus' teaching. Depend on God to help you in all situations. Do what's right. And shine your light around, helping people in need and sharing the good news about Jesus with everyone!

> Dear God, thank You for Jesus,
> the best Teacher. Help me do
> what He teaches me! Amen.

- Who is your favorite teacher at school, and why?
- What do you do to shine your light around to help others? What could you do?

GO DEEPER

What did the crowds listening to Jesus think about His teaching? Find the answer in Matthew 7:28–29.

Love Your Enemies

*"I say to you, Love your enemies and
pray for those who persecute you."*

Matthew 5:44

On Christmas Eve and Christmas Day in 1914, an amazing thing happened. Thousands of soldiers on a battlefield held a truce. They put down their weapons and sang Christmas carols back and forth to the soldiers they had been fighting. Some even gave each other gifts of food and hats. For as long as the truce lasted, these soldiers did what they could to follow Jesus' teaching to love their enemies.

We aren't soldiers fighting a war, but whenever people act like enemies to us, hurting us in any way, God tells us to show them love. As Jesus taught the people gathered on the mountainside, He said, "Love the people who are mean to you, because God loves every person. Pray for your enemies and do kind things for them."

One way children can love someone who is hurting them in some way is to tell a parent, teacher, or other adult friend and get help! Jesus does not want children to be hurt by anyone, and He wants the person doing the hurting to stop. So always speak up and get help. That is actually a kind, loving thing to do.

And pray. Pray for the neighborhood bully. For the kid who wants your position on the team. For the teacher who always seems angry at the class. For the elderly neighbor who won't let you get your softball out of his backyard. For the person who thinks you are silly to believe in Jesus. Follow Jesus' teaching, and pray for your enemies to have softer hearts and to discover how much God loves them, just as He loves you.

Dear God, thank You for always loving us whether we are bad or good. Help me love and pray for people who act like enemies toward me. Amen.

· Is anyone acting like an enemy toward you right now?
· How can you love and pray for that person?

GO DEEPER

When someone is hurtful to you, should you try to get back at them? Read Luke 6:27.

Love God, Not Money

"Store your treasure in heaven. . . . Your
heart will be where your treasure is."

Matthew 6:20–21 ICB

In a parking lot, on his way into a restaurant with his family, gold star kid Myles Eckert found a twenty-dollar bill on the ground. (A gold star kid is a child whose mom or dad has died while serving in the military.) Myles began thinking about what he could buy with the money. But then he saw Lieutenant Colonel Frank Dailey come into the restaurant in his uniform. He decided to give the money to Frank, along with a thank-you note for his service in the air force.

Myles understood the right way to use our money. It isn't just for what we need or want. It's for doing good to others too.

When Jesus taught the people sitting on the mountainside, He said, "Spend your money on what is good. Use it to help other people. Don't keep your money just for yourself. If you love God, you can't love money too."

Are you surprised to hear Jesus say we can't love God *and* money? It's true. If we keep everything we have for ourselves, we might enjoy it now, but eventually possessions wear out or break, and money gets spent or stolen. But when we do good for others with our money and possessions because we love God, it's like depositing treasure in a heavenly bank!

It's not wrong for you to have toys and games, or bikes and sports equipment, or books and music. And it's wise for you to save money for a need in the future, like going to college or buying a car. But in God's kingdom, we want to use treasure the way our Teacher, Jesus, says we should.

What are you doing with your treasure today?

Dear God, thank You for sending us a
Teacher like Jesus! Please help me obey
Him with all my treasure. Amen.

- What are some of your most special possessions?
- What could you do to help others with some of your money or possessions?

GO DEEPER

What did Jesus say about giving and receiving? Look in Acts 20:35.

Don't Worry

Your heavenly Father already knows all your needs.
Matthew 6:32 NLT

When Solomon Berg's parents bought their first house, Solomon and his two younger brothers had lots of room to run and play. There was a trampoline in the backyard, a tree just right for climbing in the front yard, and plenty of space for throwing a football. There were neighborhood friends to play with and a cul-de-sac at the end of the street for riding bikes. Everything seemed perfect.

And then Hurricane Matthew began swirling up the Atlantic Ocean near the Georgia coast, where Solomon and his family lived. They had to pack up their car and drive inland, along with more than 500,000 others just in Georgia. "When I left home,"

Solomon said, "I felt scared. I hoped the storm wouldn't make a tree fall on our house or cause any tornadoes."

Trouble comes to all of us at times. We worry about the big things that might happen tomorrow, like hurricanes and tornadoes. And we worry about the smaller things, like having to get a shot or wearing braces. But when we worry, we are forgetting that God has promised to take care of us always.

Jesus taught the people, "God takes care of all the flowers and little birds, so He will certainly take care of you! You don't need to worry! Make God and His ways the most important things in your life. Then God will give you everything you need."

God gives the flowers beautiful colors to wear. He provides food for every little bird. And you are more important to Him than all the birds and flowers. So remember what Jesus, our Teacher, said: God will take care of you in every way—you never, ever need to worry about that!

Dear God, thank You for Your love
and care always. Help me to trust
You and not worry. Amen.

- Next time you start to worry, what could you do instead?
- How are you making God and His ways the most important things in your life?

GO DEEPER

What does 1 Peter 5:6–7 tell us to do with our worries and anxieties?

Pray Like This

Lord, teach us to pray.

Luke 11:1

A four-year-old wanted to hear the same bedtime story every night. One evening, the girl's father handed her his phone instead of sitting down to read with her. He had recorded the story for her to listen to. But the little girl wasn't happy.

"What's wrong?" asked her father. "You can still hear the story. Just tap Play."

"Yes," the girl said. "The phone will read me the story, but I can't sit on its lap!"

The little girl wanted to be close to her father. God feels the same way about us. He wants us to come close and talk to him.

Jesus prayed a *lot*. Sometimes He prayed all night. Sometimes He prayed with His friends, and sometimes He prayed alone. And Jesus, in the Sermon on the Mount, taught His listeners how to pray.

First, Jesus said what *not* to do. "Don't put on a show," He said. "Don't try to impress other people with your prayers. And don't babble on and on. Instead, think about what you are saying." Then Jesus said, "Pray like this," and He taught everyone a simple prayer to use as a model, or pattern, whenever they talked with God. We can use Jesus' model prayer too! (You can find it in Matthew 6:9–13.)

God loves to hear from you! You can talk to Him anytime, anywhere, and He will hear you. He already knows what's going on and what you need, but He wants you to come and talk with Him because He loves you and He cares about even the small details of your life.

Have you talked with God today? How about right now?

Dear God, I'm so glad You want me to come and talk with You. Thank You for Jesus' model prayer. Help me pray every day! Amen.

- Who are the people you like to talk with, and why?
- What do you like about talking with God?

GO DEEPER

Where was Jonah when he prayed? Look in Jonah 1:17–2:1.

Build on the Rock

The cornerstone is Christ Jesus himself.

Ephesians 2:20 NLT

The second-tallest building in the world, the Shanghai Tower, reaches almost a half-mile toward the clouds. Inside the tower are offices, shops, a hotel, and sky-lit lobbies with glass walls. But the most amazing thing about the tower is the way it twists and spirals up to the sky.

To build such a tall, unique structure safely in the soft soil found in Shanghai required a strong foundation. Before anything was built above ground, the builders created a huge foundation underground. They drove nearly one thousand steel beams almost three hundred feet into the ground and then poured concrete twenty feet thick.

Strong wind can push a building around. Heavy rain or flooding can wash away the ground underneath it. But a building sitting on a strong foundation is safe. Tall buildings need a strong foundation, but so do ordinary houses and apartments. And so do our lives—because everyone experiences trouble of one kind or another from time to time. In a story Jesus told about two builders, He said hearing and obeying His words and teaching is the way to build a strong foundation for our lives. (You can read this story in Matthew 7:24–27).

In Bible times, building foundations were made of stone. A firm foundation depended on the first and strongest stone—the cornerstone. That's one reason Jesus is called the Cornerstone.

He is our foundation. We can build good lives by doing what He says. Then when trouble comes, we won't fall apart. Instead, we'll be like the man who built his house on the strong rock.

Are you making Jesus the cornerstone—the most important piece—of your life? How can you build your life on the Cornerstone every day?

Dear God, thank You for showing me how to have a good, strong life. Thank You for Jesus, the Cornerstone. Amen.

- What's the biggest or tallest building you have ever seen or visited?
- What are some ways we can build our lives on Jesus' words?

GO DEEPER

What else did Jesus say about His words? Look in John 14:24.

Here Is the Church

You are members of God's family.
Together, we are his house.

Ephesians 2:19–20 NLT

Maybe you know this rhyme: "Here is the church, here is the steeple. Open the doors, and see all the people!" But did you know the church actually *is* the people? It's not a building! All the people everywhere who know and love Jesus are the church. And who started the church? Jesus, the Cornerstone! His words and ways teach us how to be the church—the people living in God's kingdom wherever they are on earth.

If Jesus is your Savior, you are part of the church. You are connected to Jesus, the Cornerstone. He is the Cornerstone because He died and rose again to save us from sin, and His instructions are the church's strong foundation—they tell His followers what to do. Here are just some of Jesus' instructions for the church:

- Love one another (John 13:34).
- Serve one another (Galatians 5:13).
- Help one another (Galatians 6:2).
- Pray for one another (James 5:16).
- Teach one another (Colossians 3:16).
- Do good to all people (Galatians 6:10).
- Go and make disciples (Matthew 28:19).

Jesus is the strong Cornerstone of the church, and when everyone in the church follows Jesus' instructions, the church grows strong and does its job well.

Even though you are young, you can build up the church by following Jesus' instructions! What can you do to obey Jesus, the Cornerstone of the church, today?

Dear God, thank You for Jesus and His church. Help me always follow His instructions! Amen.

- What do you enjoy most about going to church?
- How do you follow Jesus' instructions for the church?

GO DEEPER

What did the apostle Peter say people in the church are like? Look in 1 Peter 2:5.

Wind and Waves Obey

They went and woke him, saying,
"Master, Master, we are perishing!"

Luke 8:24

When a big hurricane comes down the coast and people have to leave their homes, shelters open up for those who have nowhere to go. People stay in gyms, churches, and community centers until the danger has passed. (There are even shelters for pets!)

Jesus' disciples wanted shelter from a storm as they sailed across the Sea of Galilee one night. (You can read this story in Luke 8:22–25.) Jesus was with them, sleeping in the back of the boat. The frightened disciples wondered how He could sleep as the wind got stronger and the waves got bigger. They tried to keep the boat from sinking, but finally fear took over. They woke Jesus up, shouting, "Master! Master! We're going to drown!"

Jesus was their leader, their teacher. They had seen Him work miracles—healing people and making food multiply. They called Him Master because they knew He was in charge of things. But they didn't expect what happened next. They didn't expect Jesus to command the wind and waves to settle down. And they didn't expect the weather to obey Him. But it did!

The disciples were amazed. "Who is this really?" they said about Jesus. "Even the wind and the waves obey Him!"

We can feel the wind and hear the wind and see trees blown about by the wind. But we can't control the wind. We can see

and feel and hear the rain, but we can't control the rain. Only the Master over all of life controls the weather—storms and all.

Sometimes we feel like a storm blows into our lives even on sunny days. Something happens that isn't good, something we can't control. But Jesus knows, and He can make storms stop. Is there a problem in your life right now? Ask the Master of all to help you. He will!

Dear God, help me remember that
You are Master. You are in charge.
You will help me! Amen.

- What is the worst weather you have ever experienced?
- When you face trouble, how does Jesus calm your heart?

GO DEEPER

Is there any problem Jesus can't help us with? Read John 16:33.

Master Class

"Let me teach you, because I am humble and gentle at heart."

Matthew 11:29 NLT

If you are very talented as an actor, singer, musician, or artist, someday you might be invited to attend a master class. In a master class, students learn from experts who are performers or artists themselves. We could say Jesus' twelve disciples had a master class every day—not in music or art but in how to live.

From among all His followers, Jesus chose twelve to be His disciples. They left their homes and businesses and traveled with Jesus wherever He went for nearly three years. They watched and listened as He taught the crowds and healed the sick. They saw how He treated people with kindness and always told the truth. They saw all the ways He obeyed God's laws and how He prayed.

After Jesus went back to heaven and the church began, most of the disciples became the first leaders of the church. Jesus had chosen them to learn from Him and pass on their faith.

How wonderful it would have been to live with Jesus and learn from Him, to see Him work miracles and hear Him pray! The twelve disciples in Jesus' "Master Class of Life" were one fortunate bunch to have Him as their leader.

But we can be Jesus' disciples too! We have the whole Bible, and we learn from Jesus whenever we read its stories and teachings and promises. So be a disciple. Learn from the Master. How will you let Jesus lead and teach you today?

Dear God, I want to be one of Jesus' disciples. I want to follow Him and learn from Him. Please help me do this. Amen.

- What are some ways you learn from Jesus?
- What are some of the ways you follow Him?

GO DEEPER

What did Jesus say about students and teachers? Find out in Luke 6:40.

Never Hungry

"I am the bread that gives life. He who comes to me will never be hungry."

John 6:35 ICB

Sometimes we eat more than we should—maybe on Thanksgiving or at our favorite restaurant. Afterward we say we feel stuffed, and we joke that we'll never need to eat again. But of course our full feeling goes away eventually, and we hear our stomachs growl. We *are* hungry again.

Our bodies need food for nutrition and for energy. Jesus knew the people who had been listening to Him all day needed to eat before they began their long walks home. (You can read this story in John 6:1–15.) But only one person in the crowd had any food—a boy with just five little loaves of bread and two dried fish.

Jesus wasn't worried. He knew exactly what He was going to do. He had all the people sit in groups. He thanked God for the bread and fish. Then He broke it apart for His disciples to take to the people—and there was enough for thousands of people to eat until they were full! There was even some left over.

Jesus wanted the people listening to Him to have food for their bodies. He also wanted to teach them—and us—an important fact. "I am the Bread of Life," He said. "Listen to Me and believe. Then you will live and never be hungry." What did He mean?

Just as our bodies get hungry for food, our souls are hungry for a forever life with God. We were created to live forever with Him, but sin got in the way. Then Jesus died on the cross for our sin so we *can* live forever with God in heaven. When Jesus is our Savior, we get to fill up on His words and His presence with us every day, forever. We'll never be hungry for Him again!

Dear God, thank You for wanting me to live with You forever, and thank You for Jesus and His words and presence with me every day. Amen.

- What are your favorite foods?
- What do you think heaven will be like?

GO DEEPER

What else did Jesus say about bread? Look in Matthew 4:4.

Share What You Have

*Don't forget to do good things for others and
to share what you have with them. These are
the kinds of sacrifices that please God.*

Hebrews 13:16 GW

If you were the boy in the Bible with the five loaves and two fish, would you have been willing to give them up? Or would you have wanted to keep them for yourself?

Jesus told His disciples to find out if anyone in the crowd had food with them. Andrew found the boy with the loaves and fish and brought him to Jesus. What was the boy thinking as Jesus held up the fish and bread and thanked God?

He might have been happy and surprised to be so close to Jesus. He might have been hungry and wishing he had eaten his meal before Andrew found him. He might have been jumping up and down with excitement to get to share with Jesus. He might have been wondering what was going to happen next. He might have been feeling all those feelings all at the same time!

And then Jesus fed thousands of people with just five little loaves and two dried fish. The boy got to eat and eat until he was full, and so did everyone else. He must have been so glad he hadn't kept his small lunch just for himself.

The apostle Paul said Christians "are to do good, to be rich in good works, to be generous and ready to share" [1 Timothy 6:18]. Even if we have just a little, we can still share something with people in need. God will be sure our needs are met too. "My God will supply every need of yours according to his riches in glory in Christ Jesus" [Philippians 4:19].

So look around you, see a need, share what you have, and watch what happens!

Dear God, I want to be like the boy who shared his fish and bread with the Bread of Life to help lots of hungry people. Amen.

- When was a time others shared what they had with you?
- What do you have right now that you could share to help someone else?

GO DEEPER

Who brought gifts from believers in Philippi to the apostle Paul when he was in prison? Philippians 4:18 will tell you.

Like a Circle

He spoke to them, saying, Take courage, I Am! Stop being afraid!

Matthew 14:27 AMPC

A little boy asked his second-grade teacher, "God made everything, but who made God?" His wise teacher drew a circle on the chalkboard and said, "Like a circle, God doesn't have a beginning—or an end. He has always existed, and He always will."

That teacher was right. When Moses asked about God's name, God said, "I Am Who I Am," which means "I don't change. I always was. I always will be." Many years later, Jesus used this same name for Himself. What did Jesus mean?

The disciples learned what He meant one night as they rowed

their boat across the windy Sea of Galilee. [You can read this story in Matthew 14:22–34.] Jesus had stayed behind to pray. In the middle of the night, the disciples saw a figure walking toward them on the water. They were terrified! They thought they were seeing a ghost.

But it was Jesus. "I AM! I am with you!" He called to them. "Don't be afraid!"

Jesus existed with God before the world began. That's why Jesus could say He is I AM, just as God said from the burning bush. The same powerful, unchanging, always-existing God who spoke to Moses from the burning bush was there in Jesus in the middle of the sea, walking on water and talking to His disciples!

And just like God told Moses not to be afraid and Jesus told His disciples not to be afraid, you don't have to be afraid either, no matter what is happening. Our powerful, loving, never-changing Jesus is I AM, and He is with you always.

> Dear God, I am thankful for who You are. I will love and trust You and not be afraid. Amen.

- When do you feel afraid?
- How would remembering Jesus is with you help you when you feel afraid?

GO DEEPER

Jesus said He is I AM on another occasion. Read John 8:56–58.

Move Forward

I have heard of your faith in the Lord Jesus.

Ephesians 1:15

"On your mark. Get set. Go!" Before you run a race, go down a zip line, or start your gymnastics routine, there's a moment when you just have to go for it. You just have to move forward and be brave.

When Peter saw Jesus walking on water toward the disciples' boat, he said, "Lord, if it is You, tell me to walk to You on the water." (You can find this story in Matthew 14:22–23.)

"Come on, then," Jesus said, and Peter stepped out of the boat onto the water and started walking

As long as he kept his eyes on Jesus, Peter kept walking. But then he looked at the waves and felt the wind around him. He forgot who Jesus is, and he began to sink.

Sometimes we have to do hard things. We aren't sure we can, but we remember God's promises and we ask Him to help us. We go for it. We step out. We have faith and we start to do the task, and God keeps His promises. If we think about the difficulties, focus on our fears, or count on our own strength to get us through, we fail. But when we have faith and depend on God, He sees us through.

The best choices we make aren't always the easy choices. Studying when you'd rather be watching a movie with your friends, speaking up to stop a bully, giving your allowance to disaster relief—anything that's not easy for us to do becomes possible when we put our faith in Jesus and depend on Him.

What hard thing do you need faith or strength to do today? Be like Peter. Step out of the boat, and walk toward your goal. Then keep your eyes on Jesus, the great I Am!

Dear God, thank You that we can always have faith in You! Amen.

- What are some things that are easy for you to do?
- What are some hard things that make you nervous? How can faith help you?

GO DEEPER

A little faith can have a big effect! Read Luke 17:5–6.

Reasons to Believe

I believe; help my unbelief!

Mark 9:24

Have you ever heard of the giant lumberjack Paul Bunyan and his friend Babe the Blue Ox? The story goes that Paul Bunyan was a giant so strong he could cut down trees faster than a machine, and Babe the Blue Ox was his giant animal sidekick. Stories about Paul and Babe are fun to read, but we call them *tall tales* because they could never, ever happen. We don't have any doubts about that.

Peter walked on the water toward Jesus, but he started having doubts. People aren't supposed to walk on water, after all. And the waves were scary high. Peter's doubts took his focus away from Jesus, and Peter began to sink.

It's okay to have doubts and questions about faith sometimes. When we have doubts, Jesus understands. He's not angry with us, but He wants us to find answers. What should we do when we have doubts? One man in the Bible who asked for Jesus' help said, "I believe; help my unbelief!" That's what Peter did too when he reached out to Jesus and cried, "Lord, save me!" as he tried to walk on water.

So when you have doubts, admit it and ask for help. Tell Jesus you believe but you have questions too. Talk to your parents, your Sunday school teachers, your youth group leaders, or your grandparents. Get help looking at all the good reasons to believe.

God wants you to believe. The apostle James wrote, "If you need wisdom, ask our generous God, and he will give it to you. He will not rebuke you for asking" [James 1:5 NLT]. So keep your eyes on Jesus, I AM, who **is** always with you and ready to help when you doubt.

Dear God, help me to believe today, every day, and all my life, no matter what happens. Amen.

- What questions or doubts have you had about God?
- What can you do when you have doubts?

GO DEEPER

What did Jesus say to Thomas about believing? Look in John 20:27.

Choose Well

*In the beginning was the Word, and the Word
was with God, and the Word was God.*

John 1:1

Turn on the TV, the radio, a phone, or a tablet, and you can hear people talking any time, day or night. Printed words are everywhere too: online, in texts, in books and magazines and newspapers. Words, words, words! How do we know which words are important and true?

Jesus taught us the answer to this question when He visited Mary, her sister Martha, and her brother Lazarus at their home in Bethany. [You can read this story in Luke 10:38–42.]

Martha wanted to serve Jesus and His disciples an impressive dinner, so she hustled and bustled about in the kitchen all day. Mary wanted to hear Jesus as He talked and taught, so she went into the living room and sat down and listened. Jesus said later that Mary had chosen well. Jesus' words would be with Mary always and could never be taken away from her.

One of Jesus' names in the Bible is the Word. *Logos* is an ordinary Greek word meaning "word" or "speech" or "expression of a thought." As the Word, Jesus could show us and tell us what God is like and what God's plan is for the world. Jesus' words have life and power!

Mary sat near Jesus' feet and listened to Him talk. How do we hear Jesus' words today? The Bible is the *written* Word of God! Whenever you are reading your Bible, you are not only *hearing* about God but *meeting* with Him too. Someone has said, "The Bible is the only book whose Author is present when you read it."

Make time to read your Bible, even just a few verses, as often as you can. God loves to meet with you in His Word!

Dear God, thank You for Jesus and for the Bible—Your Word! Amen.

- Do you like to read, or would you rather listen to someone else read?
- Have you memorized any words from the Bible? Make a plan to try it.

GO DEEPER

What does Psalm 119:11 tell us to do with God's Word?

God's True Story

All Scripture is inspired by God.

2 Timothy 3:16 ICB

When you go into a library, you see picture books, novels, biographies, history books, even cookbooks and computer books. Each book is different and separate, not connected to all the other books in the library.

The Bible is a library too, but in this library the books *are* all connected. Put them together and they tell one story: the story of God's love!

The Old Testament shelves of this Bible-library hold thirty-nine books. They include books of history and law, poetry, and prophecy (*prophecy* means "about the future"). The New Testament shelves of this library hold twenty-seven books. The first four in the New Testament, called Gospels, tell us about

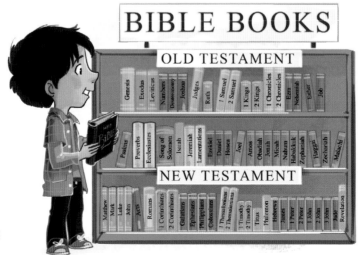

148

Jesus' life, death, and resurrection. The book of Acts is a history book about the beginning of the church. The next section of books is letters, mostly written to churches. And the last section, the book of Revelation, is a book of prophecy.

God used about forty different people to write the Bible and share His story. The apostle Paul tells us, "All Scripture is inspired by God," and, "The Scriptures give us hope and encouragement as we wait patiently for God's promises to be fulfilled" [Romans 15:4 NLT].

The Bible is a book you can read throughout your entire life. Remember, the Bible is God's written Word. It tells us who God is and what He does, so we can know Him. It tells us how to be saved and how to become the people God created us to be. It gives us strength, encouragement, and hope for the future.

Everyone loves a good story, and God's true story in the Bible is the very best story you will ever, ever hear!

Dear God, thank You for the wonderful true story of the Bible, of Your love. Amen.

- Why do you think it's important to read God's Word?
- How can you make reading or hearing God's Word part of your life every day?

GO DEEPER

What does Isaiah 55:11 tell us about the power of God's Word?

Too Busy?

"No branch can bear fruit by itself;
it must remain in the vine."

John 15:4 NIV

Both Mary and Martha were excited about having Jesus visit their home when He came to their village, but they served Him in different ways when He came.

Martha was all about the food. What should she serve for dinner? It had to be special! She got to work shopping and chopping right away. Mary was all about what Jesus had to say. He had so much to teach her! She sat down to listen and didn't move.

Martha got all upset. Why wasn't Mary helping her, doing what she was doing? She stopped her work and went looking for Mary, and when she found her, she complained, "Jesus, tell my sister to come and help me in the kitchen."

Instead, Jesus reminded her the best part of their visit was spending time with Him.

We all have different abilities, talents, and interests we can use to serve others. So the things we each do to help and serve will look different from person to person.

But no matter how we serve, we all need to spend time with Jesus, the Word, listening to Him. We can't do the good things we should if we don't stay close to Him, like branches must stay on a tree to grow fruit..

We never want to be too busy to hear Him. Jesus said Mary chose the best part—paying attention to the Word. Are you choosing the best part too?

Dear God, show me how to serve others
but always make time for You. Amen.

- What do you like to do? What are you good at?
- How can you be sure to have time in your day to spend with Jesus?

GO DEEPER

What is the right attitude for serving God? Look in Psalm 100:2.

Run to Help

*"I am the good shepherd. The good shepherd
lays down his life for the sheep."*
John 10:11

Firefighters, search and rescue teams, and police officers run toward danger when others are running away. We call them first responders. When there's trouble, they rush to help and protect. They know they are risking their own lives when they do, but they do it because they care.

Jesus cares for us. He left heaven and came to earth, knowing He would give up His life on the cross for everyone who would believe in Him. Like a good shepherd searches for a lost lamb (you can read more about this in Luke 15:1–7) or runs to save a lamb from a bear or a wolf, Jesus willingly did what it took to save His sheep—people—from sin.

Someone who didn't love his flock of sheep wouldn't try to save the sheep from trouble. He would run away instead. Jesus could have run away from His task too, but He didn't. Instead He prayed He would be able to do what God wanted Him to do.

The apostle Paul was often in danger as he traveled to preach and teach the good news, start new churches, and encourage believers to stay faithful. He was like a first responder for the church, and he said, "Imitate me, just as I imitate Christ" (1 Corinthians 11:1 NLT).

You might never be a missionary like Paul (but then again, you might!). Your life might not ever be in danger. We can't save anyone the way Jesus did, but we don't have to—He already did all that was required by giving up His life on the cross. We just need to make sure people all around us hear the good news about the Good Shepherd, who cares for us and willingly died for us.

Dear God, thank You that Jesus was willing to give up His life so I can live. Amen.

- What are some ways it is easy for you to love others?
- What are some ways it is hard for you to love others?

GO DEEPER

Are all Jesus' sheep in the same place?
Find the answer in John 10:16.

Someone's Calling

"My sheep hear my voice."
John 10:27

Right after birth (and probably before birth too), babies recognize their mother's voice. All newborns depend on their mother to feed and care for them, so it just makes sense they would know and respond to her voice more than any others.

Jesus, the Good Shepherd, said His sheep hear His voice and follow Him. Sheep depend on a good shepherd, much like babies depend on their mothers.

Sheep need help to find good food. They will eat grass right down to the roots and destroy an entire pasture if they are left in one place too long. They need quiet streams of water or they'll drink from muddy ponds instead. Sheep need protection and someone to stop them from wandering off. That's why a good shepherd trains them to listen for his voice and go where he leads.

Remember—we are Jesus' sheep! The better we know Jesus and recognize His voice, the better we can follow Him, and we won't be tricked by other voices either. "The sheep hear his voice, and he calls his own sheep by name and leads them out. When he has brought out all his own, he goes before them, and the sheep follow him, for they know his voice. A stranger they will not follow, but they will flee from him" (John 10:3–5).

How do we get to know Jesus' voice? First, listen to His words in the Bible. The whole Bible helps us know Him better. Remember that sheep *follow*. They don't run off in the opposite direction. Stay close to the Good Shepherd by spending time with Him and doing what He says. Follow the Good Shepherd, and you won't get lost.

Dear God, please help me follow the
Good Shepherd every day. Amen.

- What would make a sheep wander away from the flock and the shepherd?
- If you were a lost sheep and the shepherd found you, how would you feel?

GO DEEPER

Why do people wander away from God? Read John 3:19.

Welcome Home!

You, O LORD, are our Father.

Isaiah 63:16

It can be a lot of fun to look at photographs of your parents when they were younger. How did they wear their hair? What clothing styles did they like? What activities were they involved in?

Jesus came to show us what our heavenly Father, God, is like. He showed us God's love by what He said and what He did. And Jesus told a story about a father and two sons that helps us understand how much the Father is willing to forgive us when we do wrong. (You can read Jesus' story in Luke 15:11–32.) Sometimes we call that story the parable of the prodigal son, but really it is about the father!

When his younger son wanted to go away and spend all his money, the father knew the trouble his son would get into. But he let him go. Then every day he waited and watched for his son to come home. He saw his son coming while he was still quite far away, and he ran to him. He was so happy his son had turned away from making such bad choices and had decided to come home.

Did the father punish his son? No, the father threw a big party for him! "We have to rejoice," the father said. "My son was lost, but now he is alive again. Now he has come home!"

That is a picture of how God treats us when we turn from our sins and come back to Him. Sometimes our earthly fathers do need to discipline us to help us learn to do right. But because of Jesus' sacrifice on the cross for our sin, God the Father forgives us gladly and welcomes us home! You never need to be afraid that God the Father will punish you—He is waiting to forgive you instead!

Dear God, thank You for being our forgiving Father! Amen.

- How do you think the father in Jesus' parable felt when his son left home?
- How do you think the son in the parable felt when he was forgiven?

GO DEEPER

What does 1 John 1:9 tell us about God the Father?

All in the Family

*God decided in advance to adopt
us into his own family.*

Ephesians 1:5 NLT

Some families are big, and some are small. Some children are born into their families, and others are adopted. An adopted child becomes a permanent family member, just like the others.

In God's family, we are all adopted. The Bible says, "God decided in advance to adopt us into his own family by bringing us to himself through Jesus Christ. This is what he wanted to do, and it gave him great pleasure."

When Jesus is our Savior, God is our Father. Fathers and mothers provide for their families. They listen and teach. They give help, comfort, and encouragement for each day and for the future. And that is just how our heavenly Father treats us, His kids. "See how very much our Father loves us, for he calls us his children, and that is what we are!" [1 John 3:1 NLT].

Because we are God's children, we want to live like it! We want to thank Him for all His goodness. We can talk with Him and ask for His help. And we have the responsibility to obey Him and to love and help others the way He does. We want to be children who make Him proud! The apostle Paul tells us, "Imitate God, therefore, in everything you do, because you are his dear children" [Ephesians 5:1 NLT].

Are you living like one of God's kids?

Dear God, thank You for making me part of Your family! I'm glad to be Your kid. Amen.

- How do you feel about being in God's family?
- How should people in a family treat one another?

GO DEEPER

What does Galatians 6:10 tell us about living as part of God's family?

Alive Again

Jesus said to her, "I am the resurrection and the life."

John 11:25 ICB

When your grandparents were kids, they probably watched Saturday-morning cartoons on TV. One famous cartoon series featured the characters Roadrunner and Wile E. Coyote. Wile E. Coyote frequently got into trouble—getting hit on the head with a heavy anvil, being blown away by dynamite, or tumbling off a cliff. These mishaps should have seriously hurt him or even killed him, but he always bounced right back into action.

That's not what happens in real life. People who die don't come back.

But Lazarus did.

Lazarus had been dead for four days when Jesus arrived in Bethany. Jesus called, "Lazarus, come out!" and the dead man walked out of his tomb, fully alive. (You can read this story in John 11:1–44).

Resurrection means that something dead comes back to life. Jesus raised Lazarus from the dead to demonstrate His power over death and His power to give life. Jesus shows us how to have a good and happy life now and in the future. He said, "I came to give life—life in all its fullness" (John 10:10 ICB) and "He who believes in me will have life even if he dies" (John 11:25 ICB).

As people grow older, their bodies begin to wear out, and eventually they die. The good news is that though our bodies die, our spirits live forever. When Jesus is our Savior, we will live forever in heaven—and the Bible tells us we can look forward to brand-new bodies there too!

When you are young, you enjoy life and look forward to the future. That's how it should be. But when you hear about a believer who has died, old or young, remember that Jesus is The Resurrection and the Life. That person is safe with Him.

Dear God, thank You for Your promise of forever life because of Jesus. Amen.

• What are some things you enjoy most about your life?
• How do you think Lazarus felt after Jesus brought him back to life?

GO DEEPER

What kind of life does Jesus give us? Look in John 10:10 to find out.

Put Off and Put On

If anyone is in Christ, he is a new creation.

2 Corinthians 5:17

When a new season begins, your mom or dad might have you try on all your clothes from the year before to see what still fits. It can take a while to put everything on and take it off again.

Did you know the Bible tells us to put things on and off, just like clothes? God tells us to put *off* our sins and bad habits and to put *on* good attitudes and actions instead. When Jesus is our Savior, He gives us a new forever life—and it starts right now! But we still need to grow. We still need to learn how to live as new people who follow Jesus.

So we learn to put *off* the old . . .

But now put these things out of your life: anger, bad temper, doing or saying things to hurt others, and using evil words when you talk. Do not lie to each other. You have left your old sinful life and the things you did before. (Colossians 3:8–9 ICB)

And we learn to put *on* the new . . .

Put on then, as God's chosen ones, holy and beloved, compassionate hearts, kindness, humility, meekness, and patience. . . . And above all these put on love, which binds everything together in perfect harmony. (Colossians 3:12, 14)

Jesus is called The Resurrection and the Life not just because He could raise people from the dead, but because He rose too, and God gives us new life when we believe in Him. Then we have a lot of putting off and putting on to do. He makes us new, and we make choices to get rid of the old behaviors that don't fit anymore. It takes time, like trying on clothes. But you can do it!

Dear God, thank You for Jesus' power that helps me live a new life. Amen.

- What habit or attitude do you need to put off?
- What habit or attitude do you need to put on?

GO DEEPER

What does Colossians 3:10 tell us about our new life?

Waiting for Jesus

He first found his own brother Simon and said to him,
"We have found the Messiah" (which means Christ).

John 1:41

Waiting for your birthday. Waiting for Christmas. Waiting for your grandparents' visit. Waiting for summer vacation. Waiting, waiting, waiting. Most of us don't like to wait, but good things are worth waiting for!

God's people waited a long, long time for the One that God promised to send who would make things right again. *Messiah* (a Hebrew word) and *Christ* (a Greek word) both mean "sent one" or "anointed one."

God first promised to send a rescuer in the garden of Eden, after Adam and Eve sinned. God gave that promise again and

again through His messengers, the prophets. They said things like, "Your king is coming to you. He does what is right, and he saves. He is gentle and riding on a donkey" (Zechariah 9:9 ICB).

The Israelites watched and waited. Sometimes they forgot. But God never forgot. He knew exactly what He was going to do, and when. At the right time, God sent Jesus.

News about Jesus traveled from town to town. Was this the Christ? People listened to Him teach. They saw Him perform miracles. Crowds followed Him everywhere, and when He rode into Jerusalem on a donkey, they held a big parade. (You can read this story in Matthew 21:1–11.) The Messiah had come! This was something worth waiting for!

Still today, many people are waiting to hear that God sent Jesus Christ with the message of God's love. It's up to us to tell them—with the way we live and the words we say. So let's not make them wait any longer!

> Dear God, help me tell others about Jesus,
> the Messiah, the One You sent. Amen.

• What are some good things you have to wait for?
• What can you do to help someone who is waiting to hear about Jesus?

GO DEEPER

Why is it important to tell others about Jesus? Read Romans 10:17.

Be Ready

"Always be ready! You don't know when [I] will come."
Matthew 24:44 CEV

When you have a big event coming up at school, like field day, a picnic, or even a big test, do you sit around doing nothing while you wait for the day to arrive? No—you get ready! You might pick out clothes, gather what you need to bring, or go over what you've learned in class.

Jesus said His followers should be ready at all times for Him to return because we don't know what day it will be. He wants us to look forward with joy to when He comes again, and He doesn't want us to be surprised—He wants us to be ready.

The Bible tells us that when Jesus came the first time, the Jewish people thought He would fight the Romans who ruled them and free their land. Instead, Jesus came to die on the cross to free all people from sin—that had been God's plan all along. But God's plan didn't end on the cross. Jesus rose from the dead, and after forty days He went back to heaven. Someday He will come again—this time to rule over all!

So how do we get ready for Jesus to come back? What does that look like?

First, stay close to Him. Read His Word and listen for His voice. Pray, share, and obey. And watch for Him! Jesus doesn't want us to be lazy. He wants us to stay alert and be ready.

Some people will be afraid when Jesus comes back because they turned down His offer of salvation. But everyone who is ready will have no reason to be afraid! Instead, we will rejoice and be thankful.

Someday, whenever God says the time is right, Jesus will return to earth. You can start today to be ready!

Dear God, help me every day to be ready for when Jesus comes back! Amen.

- What's the biggest event you've ever prepared for?
- What do you do to get ready for an important event?

GO DEEPER

Jesus told a parable about being ready for Him to come. Read it in Matthew 25:1–10.

Don't Be Selfish

"Here is my servant . . . the one I chose."

Isaiah 42:1 ICB

Babies cry a lot—when they are hungry, when they're tired, when they have gas, when they need a dry diaper. They don't seem to care about anyone except themselves. But babies aren't being selfish when they act this way. They can't do anything for themselves yet, and they depend completely on others to care for them.

Jesus was never selfish. He always thought of others and did what was best for them, not for Himself. Jesus was a servant. Even though He was God, He came to serve people. The Bible says, "He didn't come so that others could serve him. He came to serve and to give his life as a ransom for many people" [Matthew 20:28 GW]. At the Last Supper, when Jesus called the bread and wine His body and blood and when He washed His disciples' feet, He was giving them pictures and reminders that He was a servant and His followers must be servants too. [You can read the story in Luke 22:7–30 and John 13:1–20.]

How can you be a servant like Jesus? Be unselfish. Someone has said, "God first, others second, I'm third." That means to focus our lives first on God, next on caring about others' needs, and then on ourselves. The amazing thing about this is that when we follow God's plan and serve others, God makes sure we have what *we* need too. He also promises that someday, in heaven, we will receive rewards for the way we served.

So rather than grabbing the last cookie, let your sister have it instead. Rather than spending all your time playing games, ask your mom or dad what you can do to help around the house. Make being a servant a habit for your life. You'll be glad you did!

Dear God, I want to be a servant and not be selfish. Please help me. Amen.

• Do you know someone who is unselfish? How?
• Why is it sometimes hard to be unselfish?

GO DEEPER

Do you want to be great? Read Matthew 23:11 to find out how.

Serve Jesus by Serving Others

"Whatever you did for one of the least of these brothers and sisters of mine, you did for me."

Matthew 25:40 NIV

At a restaurant, a server comes to take your order. The cooks in the kitchen get your food ready, and then the server brings your meal to your table. The server and the cooks all have a job to do for *you.*

As Jesus' followers, our job is to serve Him, and one way we do that is by serving *others.* That's because Jesus served others, and we want to be like Him. It's also because when we serve others, it's as if we were doing it for Him! On a future day, when Jesus returns to earth, He will say, "Whatever you did for one of my brothers or sisters, no matter how unimportant they seemed, you did for me."

So what are the ways we can serve others? Just look around! Jesus talked about making sure everyone has enough food and water. Can you donate to a food bank in your town, or help your mom or dad take a meal to a family experiencing trouble? Jesus talked about making sure everyone has the clothes they need. Do you have an extra winter coat you could give to another child who doesn't have one? Jesus talked about visiting people who feel alone, especially people who are sick or in prison. Maybe you could go with friends to a nursing home to talk or play games with the people there.

We can't do everything, but we can all do something. God gives gifts to us so we can share and give to others. Be a good servant for Jesus. Look around and find someone to help today.

Dear God, I want to be a good servant for Jesus. Please help me. Amen.

- Do you think being a servant sounds positive (a good thing) or negative (a bad thing)?
- What did Jesus think about it?

GO DEEPER

Where are Jesus' servants found? Look in John 12:26 to find out.

SAVIOR

No Fear

*Grace and peace from God the Father
and Christ Jesus our Savior.*

Titus 1:4

In baseball, when a batter gets a hit and runs to first base, an umpire is standing nearby, watching the action carefully. Runners want to hear the ump call "Safe!" and not "Out!" when they reach the base.

In a way, getting called out in a baseball game describes our lives without Jesus. No matter what we do, we just can't win against sin. No matter how hard we try, we still do wrong things. Sometimes we even *want* to do the wrong thing. We might wonder what God thinks about us because we know He doesn't want us to sin. We might imagine God is like a heavenly umpire just waiting to call us out!

But that's *not* who God is. He sent Jesus to *save* us. (You can read about Jesus' death and resurrection near the end of all four Gospels—Matthew, Mark, Luke, and John.) We have no reason to fear.

When Jesus is our Savior, we don't have to worry about what God thinks of us. When Jesus comes into our lives, He is just what we need! He gives us new life. He gives us power to say no to sin, and He gives us peace with God. And even though we have sinned (and still do), when we belong to Jesus, God says we are safe because of what Jesus did for us on the cross. "If we confess our sins, he is faithful and just to forgive us our sins" (1 John 1:9).

172

God made a way for us to have peace with Him because He loves us so much. "So now, those who are in Christ Jesus are not judged guilty" (Romans 8:1 ICB). That's what it means to have a Savior!

Dear God, thank You for my Savior, Jesus! Amen.

- What does it mean to be at peace with someone?
- Why do we want to have peace with God?

GO DEEPER

What does 1 John 4:19 say is the reason we can love God?

Saved by Grace

God saved you by his grace when you believed.
Ephesians 2:8 NLT

Flight 1549 left a New York airport on a cold January morning in 2009, with the pilot, Captain "Sully" Sullenberger, 150 passengers, and four other crew members. Shortly after the plane took off, suddenly it lost all power and began to glide downward. Captain Sully had only one way to avoid crashing into the homes, cars, and businesses below—a dangerous water landing on the Hudson River. He landed the plane safely, and everyone got out.

The passengers on the plane could take no credit for being saved from a crash—only Captain Sully. They couldn't do anything except follow his instructions as the plane went down. Sully knew what to do to save them, and they had to depend on him.

Being saved from sin—being friends with God because of what Jesus did on the cross—is a little bit like that too. We can't do to anything to save ourselves. We could never be good enough to go to heaven. God saves us because of His love and grace. [*Grace* is God blessing us even though we don't deserve it.] The Bible says, "God saved you by his grace when you believed. And you can't take credit for this; it is a gift from God. Salvation is not a reward for the good things we have done, so none of us can boast about it" [Ephesians 2:8–9 NLT].

The only thing we can boast or brag about is Jesus! He came to die on the cross so we can live with God forever in heaven. God gives us grace. He sent us Jesus. What a wonderful Savior!

Dear God, thank You for Your grace! Amen.

- Has anyone been kind to you when you didn't deserve it, and how did you feel?
- Is there someone you should show grace to today?

GO DEEPER

What is a right reason for doing good works? Find the answer in Hebrews 13:16.

Yes, Sir!

The free gift of God is eternal life
in Christ Jesus our Lord.

Romans 6:23

Officer, General, President, Queen, Your Honor, even Coach, Sir, and Ma'am. When we use someone's official title, we show them respect. We show the relationship we have with them. They have authority of some kind over us—they are our parents, coaches, government or military leaders, police officers.

In Bible times, another title of respect was *Lord*. At first, Jesus' friends and disciples called Him Lord because He was a teacher and leader. But a time came when the disciples began to call Jesus Lord because He is God. When we call Jesus *Lord*, we

are showing that He is not only our Savior who did something for *us*. He also is our Lord, the One we follow and *obey*.

When Thomas the apostle saw Jesus after the resurrection, what did Thomas say? "My Lord and my God!" (John 20:28.) (You can read about this in John 20:24–29.) Thomas wasn't convinced that Jesus was alive again until he saw Jesus. Then he believed that Jesus was the Son of God, who came to give us eternal life. And because of that, Thomas knew there was only one right thing to do—decide to follow and obey Jesus as his Lord.

We haven't seen Jesus, but we can call Jesus our Lord just as Thomas did. Jesus told Thomas, "You believe now because you have seen Me, and that's good. But those who haven't seen Me and still believe are blessed."

So if you believe Jesus is God's Son, who died on the cross and rose again, then you can say, like the disciples and Thomas, "My Lord and my God!"

Dear God, thank You for our Lord Jesus.
Help me follow and obey. Amen.

- When you receive a gift, do you have to pay for it or is it free?
- Is Jesus your Savior? Is He your Lord?

GO DEEPER

How should we respond to God's gift of grace and eternal life? Look in 2 Corinthians 9:15.

Put Faith in Action

"If you love me, you will keep my commandments."
John 14:15

Have you ever built a town with blocks, or furnished a miniature house, or set up an electric train set? With your blocks or mini-house or train set, you were in charge. You were the owner of what you made.

God is our owner. He made us and the world we live in, and He gives us everything we need for life—food and water, air to breathe, sunshine and rain. Because He made us, He has the right to tell us how to live—what is right and what is wrong. He wants us to obey Him because we love Him and because we are thankful to Him for all His blessings.

Jesus is Lord because Jesus is God's Son, and because He came to earth to save us. He is over all, and we should always do what He says. It doesn't make any sense to believe in Jesus and then not obey Him. The apostle James wrote, "What good is it, dear brothers and sisters, if you say you have faith but don't show it by your actions?" (James 2:14 NLT).

How can we show that Jesus is our Lord? The Bible has many ideas! Treating others kindly, helping those in need, praying for others, and telling people about Jesus are all good ways. Jesus said there are just two great commandments: "'You must love the LORD your God with all your heart, all your soul, and all your mind.' This is the first and greatest commandment. A second is

equally important: 'Love your neighbor as yourself'" (Matthew 22:37–39 NLT).

So obey Jesus as your Lord because you are thankful He's your Savior!

Dear God, help me remember to listen
and obey every day! Amen.

- How do we know what God says we should do?
- How do we show we are thankful to God for making us and our world?

GO DEEPER

What does James 2:17 tell us about faith and good works?

Our Best Friend

"You are my friends if you do what I command you."

John 15:14 ICB

Do you have some special friends? Where did you meet them? How did you get to be friends? Probably by spending time together and getting to know one another. Good friends make us laugh, and they love us just as we are. We can talk things over with good friends. Everyone needs good friends!

Jesus chose some special followers to be His disciples, or students, and they became His closest friends. He talked with them, and one day He said, "Now you are my friends, since I have told you everything the Father told me" (John 15:15 NLT). Jesus is your friend too, because in the Bible He has told us everything God wants us to know.

Sticking with us in good times and bad times is something else good friends do. Proverbs 18:24 says, "There is a friend who sticks closer than a brother." Jesus proved He will stick with us no matter what when He died for our sins (and then rose again!). He wants to be our friend no matter what, and He wants to talk with us about everything, good and bad. A favorite old hymn of the church puts it this way:

What a friend we have in Jesus, all our sins and griefs to bear!
What a privilege to carry everything to God in prayer!

Jesus also said His friends do what He says to do—love God, and love others. Sometimes this is easy, and sometimes it is hard. But when it's hard, Jesus gladly helps us do the right thing.

What a friend we have in Jesus!

> Dear God, thank You so much for Jesus, my very best friend. Amen.

- What do you like to do with your friends?
- What do you think makes a good friend?

GO DEEPER

How did Jesus show the greatest love anyone can? Look in John 15:13.

Friend of All

*God did not send his Son into the
world to condemn the world.*

John 3:17

Have you read *Charlotte's Web*? The novel describes the friendship between a pig named Wilbur and a barn spider named Charlotte. The farmer intends Wilbur for eating, but Charlotte writes messages like "Some Pig" in her web to persuade him to let Wilbur live. She follows Wilbur to the county fair, where he wins first place, and although she dies after laying her eggs, Wilbur watches over her egg sac. And when the baby spiders emerge, several of them stay with him as friends.

Pigs and spiders make unusual friends! Who would have expected it? But Wilbur and Charlotte accept each other, and their friendship brings them both a lot of joy.

When Jesus came, the religious leaders of the day didn't expect Him to be friends with the people they called sinners. The leaders didn't understand why Jesus hung out with "outsiders." They didn't understand that Jesus accepts everyone who will come to Him.

John 3:17 says, "God did not send his Son into the world to condemn the world." Jesus came to be our friend. The rest of the verse tells us Jesus came so "the world might be saved through him."

Jesus accepts everyone who comes to Him, no matter who they are, where they come from, or what they have done. But like the good friend He is, He wants the best for us. That's why He wants us to listen to Him and do what He says. Are you listening to your friend Jesus? He is your friend forever, and the best friend you will ever have!

Dear God, I'm so glad to have Jesus as my friend! Thank You for Jesus. Amen.

- Who have you been friends with for the longest time?
- How does it feel to have Jesus as your forever friend?

GO DEEPER

What does Proverbs 17:17 tell us about friends?

Just the Beginning

"I will ask the Father, and he will give you another Helper, to be with you forever."

John 14:16

Nobody wants a good time to end. We all feel sad at the end of a birthday party, summer vacation, or a good book or movie. We want the good times to keep on going!

After the resurrection, Jesus' disciples were so happy to see Him again! The disciples didn't want their time with Jesus to end. They didn't want Jesus to go back to heaven.

But Jesus had promised that God would send them a Helper and a Comforter, the Holy Spirit, and on the day of Pentecost, that promise came true. (You can read this story in Acts 2.) Jesus going back to heaven wasn't the end—it was just the beginning!

On Pentecost, when the church began, the Holy Spirit was available to help every believer live for Jesus. And the Holy Spirit came as a Helper not just to the first believers but also to us! How does the Spirit help us? Here are some ways:

- "The Helper will teach you everything. He will cause you to remember all the things I told you" (John 14:26 ICB).
- "The Holy Spirit will come to you. Then you will receive power" (Acts 1:8 ICB).
- "God's love has been poured into our hearts through the Holy Spirit who has been given to us" (Romans 5:5).

Jesus promised never to leave us alone, and He kept His promise by asking the Father to send us the Helper, the Holy Spirit. Let the Spirit be your helper today!

Dear God, thank You for sending us the Holy Spirit to help us live for Jesus. Amen.

- What is something you feel sad about when it ends?
- What are some things you need help with? How can you invite the Helper in?

GO DEEPER

How did the first believers experience the coming of the Holy Spirit on the day of Pentecost? Look in Acts 2:2–3.

Fruit Salad

The fruit of the Spirit is love, joy,
peace, patience, kindness, goodness,
faithfulness, gentleness, self-control.

Galatians 5:22–23

If you want a fruit salad, some work must come first. You need to buy the fruit—maybe strawberries, blueberries, and bananas or grapes, oranges, and pears. Then you peel and cut up the fruit. Put it all in a bowl and mix it together. Maybe add a little sugar or lemon juice too. *Mmm . . .* it's so pretty to look at and so good to eat!

Did you know God wants our lives to be a "fruit salad" too? He wants our lives to be like bowls full of delicious "fruit"—love, joy, peace, patience, kindness, goodness, faithfulness, gentleness, and self-control.

How do we make this kind of fruit salad? Only with the Helper, the Holy Spirit, working in our lives. And where do we get the fruit for God's fruit salad recipe? The Holy Spirit grows the fruit in us! When Jesus is our Savior and we follow and obey Him, we begin to grow the fruit of the Spirit listed in Galatians 5:22–23.

So if you dislike someone and the Holy Spirit reminds you to show love, be obedient. When you really feel like throwing a tantrum and the Holy Spirit reminds you to have self-control, follow His lead. When someone has been mean to you and the Holy Spirit reminds you to show kindness, ask Him for help to find a way.

Pay attention to the Spirit, our Helper. Then your life will become full of things even more lovely than a beautiful bowl of delicious fruit salad!

Dear God, please help me grow fruit in my life with the Spirit's help. Amen.

- What kind of good fruit of the Spirit do you have in your life and actions?
- What kind of fruit do you need to grow more of?

GO DEEPER

What does John 15:8 tell us about growing fruit in our lives?

Light Up the Dark

"I am the light of the world."
John 8:12

On November 14, 2016, people around the world saw a super supermoon—the moon looking bigger and brighter than it had in sixty-eight years! The positions of the moon, earth, and sun that day made it happen. Photographers took amazing pictures of the giant supermoon lighting up the dark sky.

Jesus said He is the Light of the World. What did He mean? Light shows us a way in the dark. Just like a supermoon lights up the sky, Jesus lights up the world. Have you ever walked into a dark room and not been sure what was there? The world can feel dark and scary when we aren't sure what's right and what's wrong, but Jesus, the Light of the World, shows us that God and His love are true.

The apostle Paul saw a bright light and heard Jesus talk to him. (You can find that story in Acts 9.)

The people who follow Jesus have a light to shine too. Jesus said the good things people see us do will cause them to praise our heavenly Father!

Our light shines the light of Jesus around too. Did you know that the moon has no light of its own? It only reflects light from the sun! When we love and honor God and do good for others, we help people see Jesus, the Light of the World. How will you shine His light today?

Dear God, please show me how to be a
shining light today and every day. Amen.

- Have you ever been outside during a full moon? What
  about when there's no moon? What's the difference?
- What are some ways you could shine a light and reflect
  Jesus' goodness to the world?

GO DEEPER

What did the prophet Isaiah say people would see? Look in
Isaiah 9:2. (Do you know who they saw?)

Not Mixed Up

*Nations shall come to your light, and
kings to the brightness of your rising.*

Isaiah 60:3

When Sheila turned seven, she invited friends to a "Crazy,
Mixed-Up, Backward Birthday Party." Sheila and her guests
wore their clothes backward and inside out! They ran relay races
backward. They ate cake and ice cream first—*under* the table.

Getting things mixed up and backward usually isn't such a
good idea! The Israelites, for example, should have understood
God's good plan is for the whole world, but they seemed to

always get that backward. They mostly thought God only cared about them. They couldn't have been more wrong.

Around the time Jesus was born, a bright new star appeared in the sky, and wise men in the East, a long way from Israel, knew it meant Jesus had been born. Maybe they had heard this prophecy: "I see someone who will come, but not soon. A star will come from Jacob. A ruler will rise from Israel" (Numbers 24:17 ICB). They traveled a long way to see the baby and worship Him. They knew that one day He would be a light for the whole world, bringing hope to all who would believe in Him.

Jesus guides us with His truth and light, and everyone in the world is welcome to come to the light and follow the light. He gave us His Word, the Bible, so we don't have to get things mixed up and backward. We know He came for everyone—not just for us, but for anyone who will search for Him!

Dear God, thank You that anyone can come to Jesus, the Light of the World. Amen.

- How is Jesus the Light of the World? In what ways does He bring brightness and hope?
- How could you help someone else find the Light of the World, like the wise men did?

GO DEEPER

What does Psalm 43:3 tell us about light and truth?

King of the Nations

He is Lord of lords and King of kings.
Revelation 17:14

Every country has some kind of government, and every government has some kind of leader, who might be called the president, the prime minister, or the king or queen. People usually look up to those leaders as powerful and important.

After Jesus fed a crowd with just five little loaves and two small fish, people began thinking He might have come from God to free them from the Romans who controlled their land. So they wanted to make Jesus their king right then! But Jesus slipped away because being crowned king of the nation of Israel wasn't God's plan for Him—even though He *was* a king.

Jesus came from the family of Israel's great King David. But Jesus came to rule over people's *hearts* by dying for their sins and then being raised to life again. Jesus came to rule over *God's* kingdom.

That's why He taught us to say when we pray, "Your kingdom come, your will be done, on earth as it is in heaven" [Matthew 6:10]. That's why He said things like "Seek first the kingdom of God" [Matthew 6:33].

But as the ruler of God's kingdom, Jesus *is* the King of kings! He is over all—higher and more important than any other leader at any time in the past, the present, or the future. And a day is coming when God's kingdom will fill the entire earth! [You can read about that day in Revelation 21–22.]

The apostle Peter tells us, "In your hearts revere Christ as Lord" (1 Peter 3:15 NIV). Is Jesus the Lord of lords and King of kings in your heart today?

Dear God, thank You for King Jesus! Amen.

- What do we call our country's national leaders?
- What makes Jesus the best leader?

GO DEEPER

What does 1 Timothy 1:17 tell us about the King of kings?

The Greatest in the Kingdom

"Let the children come to me, . . . for to
such belongs the kingdom of God."

Luke 18:16

Someone once said, "Play is a child's work." Little children learn about their world as they play—building, climbing, painting, pretending. Now that you're older, you have school and chores as part of your "work" too. The adults around you provide for you and love you, and you depend on them to take care of you. That's how it should be.

The disciples once asked Jesus, "Who is the greatest in the kingdom of heaven?" Jesus surprised them with His answer. He called a child nearby to come and stand with them. "Whoever humbles himself like this child is the greatest in the kingdom of heaven," He said [Matthew 18:1, 4].

Humble people don't think they are more important than they really are. Just like children must depend on their parents and others to care for them, people who want to be part of God's kingdom must be depend on Him too. We are humble when we depend on God and trust Him to care for us. We are humble when we thank Him for everything He does for us and everything He will do in the future.

Everyone in the kingdom of God has a wonderful, forever future waiting for them. Jesus will come back to earth as King of kings and make everything right again. There won't be trouble anymore. "There will be no more death, sadness, crying, or pain" (Revelation 21:4 ICB).

Jesus loves children, and the kingdom of God is for children too. That's why Jesus told His disciples, "Let the children come to me, and do not hinder them, for to such belongs the kingdom of God." A humble heart is full of faith and trust. Let your heart be humble before God today and every day of your life.

Dear God, thank You for Your kingdom
and the King of kings! Amen.

- Who are the people who take care of you?
- How do those people show you love and provide for you?

GO DEEPER

What will make heaven so wonderful? Read about it in Revelation 21:3.

God Has a Plan

Those who know your name put their trust in you.

Psalm 9:10

God's names tell us who He is and what He does. They tell us about His plan for the world and for each one of us too! Let's look back and think about the names you've learned about in this book.

Creator. God created the world and everything in it. He made the first people and gave them a wonderful place to live in with Him.

Sin entered the world, but **God All-Powerful** already knew what He was going to do. He began His plan by choosing Abraham, giving him a family, and promising to grow a nation from that family that would bless the whole world.

God made Himself known to that nation as **I AM**, who never changes. As **God Who Saves**, He rescued them from slavery in Egypt. As **Holy One**, He made them His special people and gave them His laws. In the Promised Land, He cared for His people as **The Lord My Shepherd** and helped them fight their enemies as **The Lord My Strength**.

At the right time, God came to live among His people as **Immanuel, God with Us**, in the form of a baby, Jesus, the **Prince of Peace**. Jesus, the **Son of God**, showed us what the **Father** is like. Jesus is the **Savior** who came to pay the penalty for the sins of everyone who would believe in Him. He rose again, and He is our **Lord**, our **Friend**, and the **King of kings** who will come back to rule over all the world.

Our God is so good! Even before He made the world, He loved us and knew just how He would save us. He always keeps His promises. He wants us to love Him and trust Him, and we can, because we know Him by name: "Those who know your name put their trust in you" [Psalm 9:10].

> Dear God, thank You that I know You by name! Amen.

- How did you get your name?
- What is one the most interesting names of God to you? Why?

GO DEEPER

What does Psalm 20:7 tell us about trusting ourselves and trusting God?

Pray the Names

Pour out your heart to him, for God is our refuge.

Psalm 62:8 NLT

You know that God always hears you when you pray. You don't need special words or a special place to pray. (Jonah even prayed from the belly of a big fish!) You can pray out loud or silently. It doesn't matter. God is with you, and He is glad to hear from you!

Sometimes, though, thinking about God's names can help us pray. We can use different names at different times, for different kinds of prayers. Here are some examples:

When we're enjoying God's colorful, wonderful, amazing world, we can thank the **Creator** for making it all.

When we're tempted, we can pray to the **God of Truth** to help us do the right thing.

We can thank **The Lord Will Provide** for all the good gifts He puts in our lives.

We can ask the **God of All Comfort** to help us when we feel sad.

We can ask the **Great Physician** to heal us when we're sick.

We can ask the **Teacher** to show us how to live in God's kingdom.

We can thank our **Savior** for saving us from sin.

We can ask the **Light of the World** to help us shine our light for Him.

At all times, no matter what is happening, we can thank God. He is **I AM**, who always has been and always will be. He never

changes. He will always be with us. We are His children, and we are so loved!

Remember His names and what they teach you. Use them when you pray, and you will keep getting to know God better each and every day!

Dear God, thank You for Your names
that help me know You better. Amen.

- What are your favorite times to pray?
- Choose one name of God. How could you use that name to pray?

GO DEEPER

What name for God is in Jesus' model prayer? Look in Matthew 6:9.

For His Name's Sake

*He restores my soul. He leads me in paths
of righteousness for his name's sake.*

Psalm 23:3

We've come to the end of this book, but throughout your whole life, you can keep getting to know God by learning about His names. He will lead you!

He will lead you in **paths of righteousness**. *Righteousness* means "pleasing to God." God will help you choose right actions and make good decisions. He will lead you by His written Word, the Bible; by the living Word, His Son, Jesus Christ; and by the Helper, the Holy Spirit.

He will **restore** your soul. *Restore* means "to give back." When you have faith in Jesus, God forgives all your sin and gives you back the close friendship with Him you were created to enjoy.

God does these things for you so you will have the best life you could ever have. He also does these things for **His name's sake**—for His good reputation. *Reputation* means "what others think of you." When God shows us His love, grace, and mercy, He shows everyone everywhere just how wonderful He is—and even more people learn to know Him and have faith in Him!

I Am, Jehovah, Yahweh, the Lord—He is our wonderful God who does not change. We want to praise Him and live so others can know him too. The Bible says,

> Kings of the earth and all people, rulers and judges of the earth, young men and young women, old men and children. Let them all praise the name of the Lord. For his name is very great. (Psalm 148:11–13 NLT)

How can you praise and honor and trust God today and every day? Every name of God gives us another reason to trust Him!

Dear God, I want to follow You always, for the sake of Your wonderful name! Amen.

- Do you have a favorite name of God today? What is it, and why?
- How has learning about God's names helped you?

GO DEEPER

What does Hebrews 13:15 say we should do because we know God by name?

Tips for Reading with Young Children

Making reading aloud to your child a fabulous experience! Here are some tips to get you started:

- Good stories are made for more than one reading. Children enjoy hearing stories again that they have enjoyed before.

- Don't be shy! Try varying your voice or adding sound effects as you read.

- Pictures help tell the story, often filling in important details. Point to illustrations and talk about them. Invite your child to tell you what's happening in a picture, how a character in an illustration is feeling, or what might happen next.

- Let your child interrupt the story to ask questions.

- Encourage your child to hold the book and turn the pages as you read.

- Try to relate a story to your child's real-world experiences, for example, "Do you remember when our family took a trip?" or, "That donkey looks like the one you rode at the petting zoo."

- Let your child read to you sometimes when he's able. A good way to do this is to take turns reading alternating paragraphs.

Learn More About the Names of God

If your family would like to learn more about God's names, here are some good books to help you get started.

FOR ADULTS

Daily Reflections on the Names of God by Ava Pennington (Revell)

Praying the Names of God and *Praying the Names of Jesus* by Ann Spangler (Zondervan)

FOR MIDDLE GRADE

God's Names by Sally Michael (P&R Publishing)

About the Author

BESTSELLING AUTHOR DIANE STORTZ loves to create engaging books based on the Bible that children want to return to again and again. Her writing goal is always making God's wonders known to the next generation.

Diane connects with parents and grandparents through her blog at DianeStortz.com and through social media, and she has become a trusted voice to help them find the best in faith-based children's books and resources. She lives with her husband, Ed, in Cincinnati, Ohio. They have two married daughters and five young grandchildren—all boys!

Diane's other books include *Say & Pray Bible*; *Say & Pray Devotions*; *Words to Dream On*; *I Am: 40 Reasons to Trust God*; *Baby, Baby!*; *The Sweetest Story Bible*; *A Woman's Guide to Reading the Bible in a Year*; and *Parents of Missionaries* (coauthored with Cheryl Savageau).

About the Illustrator

DIANE LE FEYER is a French illustrator. Even as a child, she always knew that one day she would draw wonderful pictures for kids to enjoy! She also teaches students what she knows about illustration. Diane is very busy with her life as a teacher, artist, mother, Star Wars enthusiast, and bad cook. She has two darling children, a loving husband, and a school of pearlscale goldfish in the family aquarium.

ENJOY MORE BOOKS
by Diane Stortz!

Start a bedtime Bible story tradition with your little ones tonight!

Through Bible stories with short takeaways and prayers, children will discover the meaning of God's names and just how much He loves them.

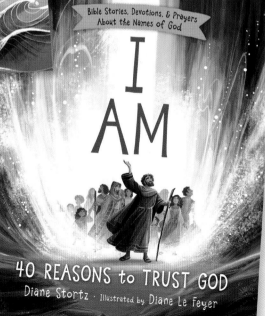